P9-EMH-193

CALLING GOD'S TOWER

... COME IN, PLEASE!

ACKNOWLEDGEMENTS

I dedicate this book to my devoted wife, Betty, acknowledging her prayers and support during my many years of traveling while she remained at home to keep everything in order.

This book was written because of my Lord Jesus Christ's Power to transform lives, such as my own. I pray that this book will encourage believers to come closer to God, and unbelievers to join the Family of God.

All incidents in this book are true, and God involved the author in each one. However, the author has sought to protect the identity of those referred to in this book, except where permission has been given. Otherwise, names have been changed.

I praise God for each one of you whom my Lord has given me as a friend and brother in Christ. Each one of you has greatly enriched my life.

CALLING GOD'S TOWER

... COME IN, PLEASE!

by Coach Floyd Eby

DISTRIBUTORS
A Division of Baker Book House
Grand Rapids, Michigan 49506

CALLING GOD'S TOWER...COME IN, PLEASE!

ISBN: 0-8010-3382-9

First printing, November 1975
Second printing, April 1976
Third printing, April 1977
Fourth printing, April 1978
Fifth printing, April 1979
Sixth printing, June 1980
Seventh printing, August 1981
Eighth printing, August 1982
Ninth printing, August 1984

OTHER BOOKS BY THE AUTHOR
MIRACLES OF LOVE
CHAMPIONS FOREVER

Printed in the United States of America

INTRODUCTION

This is a book about God's Power. The purpose of this book is to give personal evidence of that power through the transformation of many lives with which the author has been involved. The author completely realizes that none of this was of his doing, but completely through God's Love, Compassion and Power. The author was just fortunate to be used as a vehicle or instrument of God to present this Wonderful Way of Life to many people who needed to come to Jesus. The author also realizes that each one that came to know Jesus, was prepared by God through His Holy Spirit.

God has opened many doors in many areas: churches, schools, jails, hospitals, sanitariums, mental institutions, homes, communes, hitchhikers, flying, business, neighbors, friends, relatives, professions, Bible studies, courts, clinics, crusades, athletics, speaking engagements, buses, trains, marriages, divorces, problems, hotels and motels, and personal contact, whenever God opened the door.

The author prays that this book will be used of God to bring unbelievers into the Family of God, to stimulate believers to be used of God in spreading the Good News of a Wonderful Saviour, to help believers to get closer to God, and to give believers more assurance of God's Wonderful Love, Compassion and Power.

The author has convenanted with his Lord, that all monies derived from the sale of this book will be used one hundred per cent in the Missionary Work of our Lord Jesus Christ. God has already taken care of his daily needs.

If God has in some way used this book to help you, either as an unbeliever becoming a believer, or as a believer becoming strengthened in the faith, or as a believer being used of God in telling others; the author invites you to write to him or telephone him and he will put you on his prayer list. If you send a picture of yourself, the author will put it on his prayer board. The author will also try to visit you as his Lord opens the door, and makes time available. There is absolutely no cost or obligation to any of the above, as it has already been paid for by the atoning blood of Jesus on the Cross. May our Lord bless you as you read this book. All correspondence to be mailed to:

Floyd Eby
15 Cardinal Drive
Coldwater, Michigan 49036

Unworthy, but His,

Floyd Eby

CONTENTS

ABOUT THE AUTHOR

"ON THE WINNING TEAM"

Coach Floyd Eby pictured with his 1949 State Basketball Championship Team of Coldwater High School of Coldwater, Michigan.

The team members now include two dentists, an ordained minister, a teacher and coach, two high ranking Army Officers, a pharmacist, a university science instructor, two outstanding business executives and three successful businessmen.

Coach Eby pictured below as he appears now in serving His Lord Jesus full time as speaker, evangelist, missionary, lay witness, counselor, Gideon distributing the Word of God, and producer and director of a daily Christian television program: "Free Ticket to Heaven." The television program includes the teaching of God's precious Word, testimonies, music, interviews, etc. Coach Eby also holds Bible studies in homes. Coach Floyd Eby has a wife, Betty, two daughters and four grandchildren.

Coach Floyd Eby has been credited by many coaches and fans as the originator of the basketball full court zone press, "race horse" basketball, and the one handed jump shot as early as 1939. Coach Eby was also the originator of the football open huddle, defensive huddle and the split T offense.

God has guided Coach Eby into many endeavors:

1.) Master of Science degree plus ten credits toward a Doctorate from Michigan State University at East Lansing, Michigan.

2.) Taught Science 30 years in the secondary public schools of Michigan. Selected Teacher of the Year in the State of Michigan in 1965.

3.) Coached 25 years as head coach in basketball, and other sports such as football, baseball, and track for a lesser number of years. The coaching career included many championships, including two State Championships in basketball, but even more important included so many opportunities to witness for his Saviour to so many young people.

4.) State President of the Michigan Gideons for three years.

5.) Two years overseas in the United States Navy during World War Two as Communications Officer on a Destroyer Escort.

6.) He flies his own plane approximately 60,000 miles per year, and the Lord has given him the opportunity to give over 200 messages each year including athletic banquets, church banquets, Junior and Senior high schools, college groups, pulpit supply and Gideon messages throughout the midwest.

7.) He has also been engaged in many business enterprises: Cablevision, Building Contracting Business, Modular Homes, Mobile Homes, Financing, Sub-division, Insurance, Real Estate, Sports Announcer, and Frozen Foods. The above made it possible for him to serve his Lord, and pay his own way with funds supplied by his Lord through the above enterprises.

8.) He has also had the opportunity to work with over 3000 people in the Midwest and other states: telling about God's wonderful plan for their lives, seeing them join the Family of God, and then follow-up with them with visits, letters and phone calls, as well as home Bible studies to encourage them to grow spiritually. He has over 3000 people on his prayer list.

9.) Selected for State High School Coaches Hall of Fame in 1964.

10.) Elected Outstanding Citizen of Coldwater, Michigan, his home town, in 1976 by the Greater Coldwater Area Chamber of Commerce.

*"And I said, Oh that I had wings like a dove:
for then would I fly away, and be at rest."*
Psalms 55:6

1

FLYING WITH GOD

Blue Angels

I was flying my Cessna 172 Skyhawk to Florida with my son-in-law, Bob, and two other adults and a child. Upon arriving at Talahassee, I established a flight plan to Ocala to Orlando. When we were about 25 miles from Ocala, I noticed some jets "buzzing" around the airport area. "Do you see those crazy Army jet pilots cutting capers ahead of us?" I asked Bob. "They aren't supposed to be doing that."

The jets soon disappeared, and I thought there was no further problem, so I proceeded on my originally planned course over Ocala. But just as I reached the Ocala airport, six army jets poured in on me. They were the Blue Angels Thunderbirds, now beginning an air exhibition. The first time we had spotted them, they had been looking the area over in preparation for the exhibition. Now, the exhibition was on.

I called the Ocala airport. "Ocala, this is Cessna 5750 Romeo. What is going on here?"

"Get out of here!" They screamed at me on the radio.

Ocala also gave me a frequency to call. It was McCoy Air Force Base in Orlando. They also ordered me out of the area --but quick!

I was trying my best, but my Hawk's 130 miles per hour seemed awfully slow compared to the jets' 600 mph.

Four jets were flying in formation with two others doing special tricks.

"Pop, here come four right under us!" shouted Bob.

Whish. were they ever going fast! There must have been 10,000 people on the ground watching the performance thinking we were the clown in the act. I don't believe they knew they were watching the first Blue Angels show in history with a Skyhawk in it. The six jets continued to buzz over and under and around us as I continued to try and maneuver us out of that precarious situation. After a few minutes, which seemed like eternity, we found our way clear and headed toward Orlando. The fact that the Orlando Television station played the performance back on television the next day pointing out the Skyhawk being flown by a clown did very little to help my ego as a flyer.

After arriving back home in Michigan, I told my flight instructor about the incident. When he started "chewing me out," I informed him it was not my fault. I had established a flight plan at Tallahassee over Ocala to Orlando, and they failed to notify me of the restricted area. Anyway, I told him I wasn't even scared, because I knew that those jet pilots knew what they were doing, and that they were just trying to scare me by coming close.

"Those pilots didn't even see you," he responded. "They only watch their instruments and the plane adjacent to them, because they know the air is officially cleared." I then became frightened thinking about what could have happened.

A month later, we were having one of these very same Blue Angel Shows at our own local airport. As I watched them doing rolls and other tricks at 600 mph, and pictured my Skyhawk up in that mess, I got the chills again. When I went to sleep that night, I dreamed about being in that show, and I saw a jet on my port bow. I turned my wheel hard and quickly to the starboard and flipped myself right out of bed, landing hard on the floor.

I woke up in a hurry. My wife from the bed asked, "What---what happened?"

"I just missed a jet," I replied from the floor.

Flying blind

After completing my solo flight, my instructor told me I could fly by myself in good weather, and to stay around near the airport, but under no circumstances could I take anyone up with me unless he was a registered pilot. I had already purchased my own plane, which I was now learning in, but I had had absolutely no under-the-hood instrument training. In fact, I knew nothing what so ever about instrument flying.

I had some business to take care of in Saginaw, Michigan, and decided to take my plane rather than drive. By the time I had flown 20 miles, I ran into a low cloud ceiling of perhaps 800 feet. I knew I was supposed to have at least a 1,000 foot ceiling. I decided that I had to either turn back or go up through the clouds until I broke out up on top. I had heard pilots talk about how beautiful and clear it was up on top, so I decided to go up rather than turn back.

I didn't know that if you fly into clouds without being on instruments, you will be involved in a death spiral within 18 seconds.

I pulled back on the wheel and started up through clouds paying no attention to instruments which I knew nothing about. I flew at least 15 minutes up through those clouds until I broke out on top at 8,500 feet, and I thought it was just beautiful as I could see 50 miles in every direction except down which was nil.

I then began to wonder how I was going to get down.

I did realize that when I started down, if the clouds were too close to the surface of the earth, that I would crash before I could pull out. I called Lansing, and asked if there were any breaks in the cloud formation toward Saginaw. The answer came back negative. I did not realize at the time that God had protected me for 15 minutes against natural aerodynamics, but I now started praying to God for a hole in the clouds. About 20 miles from Saginaw, I spotted a large hole on my port bow about 15 miles away, and I scooted through this hole in about 7 minutes and landed at Saginaw.

As I related this incident to my son-in-law, Bob, he exploded, "Pop, don't you know better than to go through clouds without instruments, and that you could have crashed some 18 seconds later?"

Once again, I found that my God still had work for me to do on this earth. Praise His Holy Name!

No Myth

My daughter, home from college, presented me with this situation. "Dad," she said, "this fellow at college makes fun of my Christian belief. He says that Christianity is a myth; just a matter of the mind of what you want to believe. It is just a psychic myth. What would you tell him?"

I told my daughter that I would tell him what happened to me one night at Gaylord, Michigan. On Friday, I flew my plane with my wife to Harbor Springs to be present at a meeting at Petoskey, Michigan. The next morning it was foggy, so my wife and I rode down to Gaylord with some friends, for meetings on Saturday. After the evening banquet, one of my friends was flying his plane back to his home at Hillsdale, Michigan. I asked my friend if he would first fly me up to Harbor Springs so I could fly my plane back to Gaylord in order that I would have it available to fly home on Sunday. Howard, his friend and I departed Gaylord about 11:00 p.m. Some fog was starting to roll in then, but I thought I would be back in 45 minutes, before the fog became bad.

Howard left me at the Harbor Springs airport, and took off for home. I warmed my plane up, and departed for the short stretch to Gaylord. As soon as we were airborne, I talked to Howard on the interplane frequency. When my instruments indicated I had arrived over Gaylord, I found the airport completely fogged in. I was above the fog, but I could not see the town. It was impossible to land.

I radioed Howard, asking how his homeward flight was progressing. "Terrible," he informed me. He was turning back to Gaylord.

It wouldn't do any good, I radioed. Gaylord was closed in. I was circling above it, trying to decide what to do.

Howard told me to wait a few minutes, and he would soon be back, and we would call other airports hoping for one not fogged in. I told him to hurry because I had only one hour of fuel remaining.

I kept circling Gaylord above the fog watching for Howard's plane. It flashed past, and I told him on the radio not to come so close. We had determined that we could land at Traverse City.

* * *

As I had been circling above the fog, I paid no attention to my instruments, but suddenly I had dropped into the dense fog. I heard my motor racing, and knew I was headed at the ground, and I was completely disoriented.

I immediately tried to go on instruments, but they were spinning like I had never seen before.

Because of this and the motor racing, I knew I was in a death spiral for the first time.

I looked at my speed indicator and it read 180 mph. I was helpless, and I knew within just a few seconds I was going to crash and go into eternity. I remember saying to my Lord, "I know no way to pull out of this Lord, and I am coming Home."

No more had I uttered this and I saw street lights, and I said, "Lord, level off my wings if you desire, and I will pull this wheel back as hard as I can, and everything is in Your hands."

Within seconds my Skyhawk was flying back up through the fog with wings leveled, and with no damage---but just missing the streets of Gaylord.

Howard was on the radio screaming, "Where are you? Where are you?"

"Please, buddy, head for Traverse City," I requested. "And

go slow enough so I can follow you, because I just really had a real encounter with my Saviour, and He is now my pilot forever."

Sometime later we landed at Traverse City with a few minutes of fuel left. I called my wife, who had been waiting at the Gaylord airport when I almost crashed at her feet.

Daughter, tell this fellow at your school that my God is not a myth, but is a wonderful performer of miracles. Tell him that aerodynamics had me in the grave until my Saviour interceded. You see, when in a death spiral, you must level off your wings before pulling back on the stick. Otherwise, pulling back on the stick just tightens the spiral and makes it worse. Also, tell this fellow that the Cessna Aircraft Company insists that a Skyhawk headed directly at the ground at 180 mph must have the stick pulled back very easy and steadily.

Any abrupt change will certainly tear the wings off at that speed. You see fellow, no myth, but God leveled the wings, and kept them attached to the plane while I did everything to cause it to crash. If Christianity was a myth of the mind, I would not be here writing this book, but would be decaying in a grave with no hope. But you see fellow, I know I have a place prepared for me, when my Lord decides to allow me to come Home!

Faith Is Needed To Fly

Jim, one of my coaching friends, decided to fly with me to Holland for a meeting. As we arrived at the local airport, the weather looked much worse than the Flight Service Station had reported. As we gassed up the plane, one of my pilot friends shouted at me, "You aren't going up in this stuff, are you?" "I am going to Holland," I replied, "My weatherman said it was going to be all right." My friend told me I must be checking the wrong weatherman. As this conversation was going on, my friend, Jim, stood around looking dubious.

After departing from runway 21, the weather was marginal until we came within 40 miles of Holland, and then it started raining hard with strong winds and poor visibility. I had never landed at Holland before, at night. Therefore, I came in extra high to be sure I wouldn't fly into some tower or smokestack. The wind was a crosswind coming off Lake Michigan with sheets of rain at about 40 mph.

As I started letting my Hawk down on the runway, fighting the crosswind, I found myself too high and running out of runway. However, I decided I could make it and continued to down the plane as rapidly as possible without flaps because of the crosswind. I planned on hitting the brakes at touchdown. I landed with less than half of the short runway left.

As I hit the brakes, the plane was bouncing and the brakes only helped when the wheels would touch the runway. I finally came to a screeching halt at the very end of the runway, just before sliding into a highway crowded with many speeding cars. As the plane stopped, Jim immediately jumped out and headed for the terminal building.

At the end of the meeting, eighteen men joined hands in a circle, including Jim and me, and several men prayed. Each one prayed for our safe return to Coldwater through this bad weather. I believe this made Jim more apprehensive than ever about the return trip.

When a friend took us to the airport, it was raining and blowing even more. I told Jim that we would take off, and if it was as bad upstairs as down below, we would come right back down and stay overnight.

I had a hard time lifting the Hawk off the runway with that stiff crosswind, and heavy sheets of rain. In fact, the stall horn blew and I didn't think we were going to make it, but we finally did get airborne, when a blast of wind and rain struck us and almost tipped us over.

Jim shouted above the noise, "I don't think we should be up here in this mess!"

"I don't either," I shouted back, "We will go back down."

As I made the turn to the left, I could see lights to the southeast at least 5 miles. I told Jim we would try it for only a few miles, and would not leave the sight of Holland lights unless the weather improved. The weather steadily improved, and was soon good flying weather the rest of the way home.

I then started talking to Jim about my faith in God. "You know, Jim, you might think this Christian meeting tonight was made up of a bunch of religious nuts or fanatics," I pointed out. "But many of that group of men were some of the outstanding citizens in Holland, including well-to-do businessmen, educators, professional men, and they believe just like I do because we all read the same Bible."

Jim didn't comment, but I knew he was thinking.

Jim and I were flying to Florida one night over the mountains of Georgia. We were up about 1½ miles on a clear night at 2:00 a.m., and I was becoming sleepy. I looked over at Jim and noticed him dozing. I started dozing also, but woke up in a hurry when Jim poked his elbow into my ribs. Jim did not sleep anymore, and every time my head went down, his elbow would strike me in the ribs. When we arrived at Tallahassee, Florida, my right rib cage was plenty sore.

Flying back from Florida over the mountains in Tennessee, we ran into a low ceiling just above the mountains. Flying just below the clouds, we were close enough to the mountains to be affected by the downdrafts. It was a very rough, turbulent ride. Skimming along below the clouds, I suddenly found us enveloped by clouds, and immediately went on instruments. Jim grabbed the strap above his head and exclaimed, "I don't like this!" "Then get out, Jim," I replied. But Jim stayed on board.

When Mountains and Clouds Meet

I departed from Tallahassee, Florida one day with my wife, and youngest daughter, Pat. I checked the Flight Service Station about the weather to Rome, Georgia. The weather was O.K. within a few miles of Rome, which at the time was enveloped in a heavy rain storm, but was predicted to move out of the area within the hour. Since my ETA at Rome, Georgia was two hours away, I reasoned that I would have no trouble landing at Rome.

Two hours later as I passed over the Rome Omni Station and headed for the airport which was located down in the valley, I flew into a heavy rain storm and low cloud formation. I knew that I should immediately do an 180 degree turn and fly back into the good weather I had just left, but I heard on the radio there was a plane in that direction. I decided to stay on my present course for a minute or two until it cleared my proposed path. By that time, I was completely lost and flying down a valley with mountains on both sides with the tops of the mountains enveloped in clouds. I called Rome on the radio which is not a controlled field, and told them about my predicament, and the man on the radio suggested I try to go through some holes in the clouds, and get on top and fly south where the weather was good. I saw a few holes, and started up. About the time I would reach a hole, it disappeared, and I had to look for a new one. Finally all holes disappeared, and I was flying blind, and the man suggested I come down. I knew I was in serious trouble, because if I didn't break out into a valley, I would crash into the top of a mountain.

I decided that I would have to take the chance, I did, and Praise God we broke into a valley. Once again, flying through a valley of heavy rain, I talked to Rome, and the man now recommended strongly that I make an emergency landing right now in the valley. I replied, "Negative." He then said he was calling the Military Air Force at Atlanta, Georgia and they would send out a plane with radar, locate me and lead me in.

As we flew back and forth in the valley, we tried to identify our position to Rome. My wife was praying, and my daughter, Pat, was reading a book -- apparently unaware of the seriousness of this situation. I called her attention to the importance of helping me identify our position. Finally, Rome became aware of our location when we spotted a freeway, railroad track, and river all running the same direction. Rome told me to circle a cloverleaf of the freeway, and they would send a plane up and lead us down the proper valleys to the airport, which they did.

After a couple of hours waiting, the weather cleared and we departed Rome. Arriving over Kentucky, the weather once again forced us to find a place to set down. I spotted a blacktop strip on the top of a mountain with a city in the valley. I landed, but could not locate any phone or help, so after another two hour wait, we took off and flew on home. I found out later that we had landed at Harlan, Kentucky.

A Captive Audience

Although my plane is noisy, I have sometimes found it is a good place to witness for my Lord. They don't get out on you, and they are in a frame of mind to listen. One night my friend, John, flew with me to Detroit for a meeting. We were landing at Berz Airport in suburban Detroit. Even though it was clear that night, I could not spot the airport among all those thousands of lights. We talked to the airport on unicom, and found out there were also three other planes up in the sky trying to locate the same airport. John was quite excited about this, but we finally made it down. Flying back to Coldwater, after the meeting, John asked me some questions about my message. After we landed and were sitting in my pick-up truck, I told John about God's wonderful Plan for his life, gave him a Bible with the verses underlined, and told him to go home and get right with God before he went to bed. He did, and later his wife also joined the Family of God, and both have become two of my wonderful Christian friends with whom I meet weekly, and we study the Scriptures together. I praise God for them!

It Pays to Believe

My friend John and I, and my Pastor, flew to Alpena, Michigan one evening for a meeting. Arriving back at the Alpena airport after the meeting, we checked the flight service station for the weather to Coldwater, Michigan. Apparently it was marginal VFR the entire trip, but the weatherman notified me that he would have the next report in at midnight, in 15 minutes. Being anxious to get started, we took off. We were bucking a 40 mile head wind, and halfway between Alpena and Saginaw, it started to snow as well as rain.

I called the Saginaw tower and requested their current weather. They reported freezing rain, and wanted to know if we were icing up yet. I gave them a negative answer, and told them I would keep in constant communication with them. It was a black night, and we were over a lonely uninhabited area with no lights showing from the ground.

We kept flying through the rain and snow to Saginaw without icing up, praise God, and when we reached Saginaw, the weather had cleared up. Calling the Tower again, we received a new weather report of current weather from Saginaw to Coldwater which was now back up to marginal VFR, with only slight reported rain in Battle Creek, so I decided to fly home.

Approximately 50 miles southwest of Saginaw, I flew into a rainstorm. Because it had not been predicted, I reasoned that it would be only a brief and scattered shower. I would soon be through it. However, the farther we flew, the worse the storm became. We were soon lost, not knowing our exact position.

The outside thermometer indicated 31-32 degrees, freezing rain. Pastor Arthur, sitting in the co-pilot seat, with John in the back, kept watching the temperature carefully. I could no longer see ahead; only lights down below us on the ground. I came to a fair-sized town and started circling it to look for a lighted airport because I was certain that we would ice up at any time and be forced to land. A small amount of ice on the external surface of the plane will force it down since it doesn't have the necessary power to carry all the extra weight.

I could not locate a lighted runway, so I called the Lansing Tower, and told them I was lost and in a predicament. I was circling a town, but couldn't find any airport.

"50 Romeo, this is Lansing Tower. Key your mike to our frequency, and we will give you a fix, and tell you what town you are circling."

I did as requested.

"50 Romeo, this is Lansing Tower. You are over St. Johns, Michigan and they have no lighted airport."

"Lansing Tower. This is 50 Romeo. I have tuned into your Omni and am flying directly to your airport."

"50 Romeo. Lansing Tower. Negative. Do not fly to Lansing Airport."

"Lansing Tower. 50 Romeo. I have to land at your airport...I have no other choice. I am in serious trouble and will crash if I can't set down soon. You are the closest."

"50 Romeo. Lansing Tower. No way can you reach our airport. It is impossible for you to land at Lansing in this freezing rain without crashing. Try Saginaw."

All this time I had been circling St. Johns on instruments, and talking on the radio...I was busy.

I called Saginaw Tower. "Saginaw Tower -- this is Cessna 5750 Romeo. I am over St. Johns, Michigan. I request permission to land at Tri-City Airport. I am in trouble -- Over."

"50 Romeo. Saginaw Tower. Negative. It is impossible to land at Saginaw. Try Flint!"

"Flint Tower. This is Cessna 5750 Romeo over St. Johns, Michigan. I am in trouble with freezing rain. Request permission to land at Bishop Airport. Over."

"5750 Romeo. Flint Tower -- your request is almost impossible, but you can try. Turn to heading on radial of 090 on Flint Omni. Over."

By this time I thought I was headed on radial 090 on Flint Omni. I checked my gyro compass heading again and I was going the exact opposite on 270...due west instead of due east.

I concentrated on my instruments, and was soon headed on radial 090.

"Flint Tower. 50 Romeo. I am now on radial 090. How close will this course bring me to the Owosso Airport?" I could feel the weight of the ice forming on my plane and I just knew there was no way I could reach Flint.

"50 Romeo. Flint Tower. If you stay on radial 090, you should pass two miles south of the Owosso Airport. We will call the sheriff's department and have them check the Owosso runway lights to be sure they are on. Over."

I was still flying at 3,000 feet, but now had to open up my throttle full, and I was still losing altitude. I knew it wouldn't be long before we crashed into Eternity unless our Lord opened up the Owosso Airport soon.

Down to 2,000 feet, now 1,500 above sea level -- only 600 feet above the ground surface.

Praise God. On my left was the Owosso Airport with a lighted runway running east and west.

"Flint Tower. 50 Romeo. Have spotted Owosso runway. Which would be best; runway 27 or niner?"

"50 Romeo. Flint Tower. It makes no difference. You have a 40 mph crosswind from due south, correction, 50 Romeo...You should try landing on 27 coming from the east, because there are fewer obstacles if you crash. Over."

I turned the Hawk on a left base for runway 27, and we were sinking fast. I turned on short final with full throttle, and ice came over all my windshield.

I could see nothing forward, but could only look out the side window.

I knew the runway had to be a glare of ice, but I had no idea if I was lined up properly, or if I was going to reach the end of the runway before touchdown.

I said, "Lord, we are completely in your hands. There is nothing more I can do."

We touched down right at the beginning of the runway, and directly on it even though I could see nothing. I didn't brake for at least 2,000 feet, then worked the brakes just slightly. When we stopped, we were at the very end of the runway.

As we sat there, I looked over to Pastor Arthur and he exclaimed, "No one, but no one, can say that God doesn't answer prayers!"

I taxied off the runway by sticking my head out the side window, stopped, and got out. There was one-fourth inch of ice all over the entire surface of the plane, including the windshield. We cleared off the windshield and taxied up to the motel, rented a room and stayed overnight.

The next morning we were able to fly home. That night at prayer meeting, I told Pastor Arthur that I almost didn't come. He said, "Why not?" I answered, "Because I thought you would be all prayed out."

I really was happy that Arthur was with us. I know God answered his prayers.

Don't Take Off Without God

I picked up Del and Bob, two new Christians, and drove to the airport. It was 6:00 a.m., still dark and looking hazy around the lights. The weatherman had forecast marginal VFR, and we were headed for a seven o'clock prayer breakfast in Ann Arbor, Michigan. We pulled my Skyhawk out of the hangar, and took off on runway 21. When we climbed to 300 feet, everything disappeared from sight ... we were completely enveloped in fog or low cloud formation. I immediately went on instruments, and even though now flying blind, I tried to stay in the airport pattern. Then I realized I was in a precarious position, and could fly into a tree, house, smokestack or tower at any moment. I climbed through the "soup" up to 2,000 feet and broke out on top.

The immediate danger was now past, but I had another serious problem.

As we started on the course for Ann Arbor, I called Jackson Tower and found out that Jackson, Willow Run, Ann Arbor and Detroit were all fogged in. I changed course for Battle Creek, and when within radio range, I contacted the tower, but they were also fogged in. They thought possibly Grand Rapids was still open. I had still another problem. The night before, I had flown my plane in from a two hour trip, and therefore my gas was half gone when I took off from Coldwater. Not wanting to get lost, I beamed in to the Battle Creek Omni, and while passing directly over the Battle Creek

Airport, according to my instruments, there was a hole in the cloud formation which looked directly down on their big runway. I called the tower and asked permission to land, but they refused, stating that the official time of sunrise was still 15 minutes away and that the visibility was too low to allow a special VFR to land at night. By then, I had determined that Grand Rapids was my best bet as they were still open, but I was fast running out of fuel. I headed toward Grand Rapids. After 8 minutes of flying, I suddenly realized that by the time I flew back to Battle Creek, it would be official sunrise, and I then could scoot down through that hole and land at Battle Creek.

When I reached Battle Creek, the hole had disappeared.

I now had only one alternative left. I needed to get to Grand Rapids, and pray that they would still be open and that we would not run out of gas. This was the first time Del had ever been in an airplane, but praise God we made it. We were able to attend a prayer breakfast in Grand Rapids that morning.

Orders from the Tower

I flew to the large Kansas City Airport one night at midnight with one other passenger. I contacted the tower when I was still 25 miles out, and eventually they notified me to follow a four motor jet into the big runway. These large jets were landing one after the other. I located the one I was supposed to follow, coming in from the north, as I was flying in from the east. When I reached left base, I slowed my airspeed to 80 mph and soon turned on to final, following the jet passenger plane at the proper distance. There was quite a lot of static on the radio as I listened to the tower continue to give instructions. I heard the tower call the jet behind me, telling him that he was getting too close to the Cessna in front of him. The jet answered, "I can't help it, I am going as slow as I can."

"50 Romeo, this is the tower, increase your speed."

I kicked my speed up to 90 mph.

A minute later more instructions came. "50 Romeo, left 360."

Because of the static, I wasn't sure he was talking to me, or if he was talking to the jet behind me. The left 360 meant for one of us to circle to the left immediately, making a whole circle turn.

I couldn't execute the maneuver until I was certain it was for me, even though by now, the jet ahead of me had already touched down, and I was coming close to that huge lighted runway. It looked so inviting compared to a left 360 and a good chance of hitting some buildings, trees or towers.

"Tower, this is 50 Romeo. Were you talking to me?"

"Yes, you! 50 Romeo!" The tower screamed.

I knew the tower was considering the balance of two lives lost in a Cessna compared to a couple hundred in the jet. However, I was tempted to declare an emergency and land anyway, but I knew I would lose my license. I pushed the throttle in full, and made a sharp turn to the left, pulling back on the stick as much as I dared without stalling.

Fortunately, we skimmed over the buildings and trees which we could not see in the dark and completed the left 360 turn following the next jet in to land.

About six months later, I was flying out of this same Kansas City Airport on a very hot, humid day about noon. Of course, regulations call for less weight in the plane on a hot day, because more power is needed to lift the plane from the

runway. My wife, youngest daughter, and her girl friend were with me plus a couple hundred pounds of luggage. I knew we were overgrossed greatly for such a hot day, but expected the tower to order us to depart on the large jet runway. However, this time the tower ordered us to a shorter runway, and was coordinating our takeoff with the jets on the large runway. As the tower gave permission, I pushed the throttle in full and held it down on the runway while the plane slowly picked up speed. I knew my chances of not stalling and crashing would depend on how much speed I could negotiate before I ran out of runway. As I was reaching the end of the runway, I pulled off at 80 mph. I had another problem immediately. Obstacles such as buildings had to be cleared. The Skyhawk was just about holding its own without gaining much altitude.

I was only about 30 feet off the ground when the tower came in. "50 Romeo, start a left turn and go up the valley."

No way would I be able to turn at this altitude without my low wing striking an obstacle. I didn't dare turn sharp because of the load, heat and lack of speed and power.

I pretended not to hear the tower, and didn't answer. I was busy picking out the direction of the lowest one story houses and other obstacles. When I cleared the smallest houses and buildings, I started a gradual turn to the left and headed over downtown Kansas City. The tower was concerned with the larger jets and seemed to have forgotten about me, and I was praising God I was on my own. By now I had reached the large downtown buildings, and was flying between them. We could actually see into the windows of these large buildings as we passed by. However, I was able to guide my plane between the tall buildings ahead, and then made another turn to the right, going home.

Now Hear This, I Am a Minister

In the sixties, our Junior High School science department was preparing for an egg drop from an airplane to simulate the landing of a man on the moon. Each student could box up an egg following certain rules to insulate or improvise methods of packing to prevent the breakage of the eggs on ground impact. Many different ideas came forth, including such things as having a small parachute come forth during the fall to lessen the impact; the use of foam rubber, springs on the bottom of the box, etc. I was selected to be the pilot and furnish the airplane to take these packages up and push them out. Our football coach, Roy, was to unload the packages at a given signal from the pilot.

Much publicity was received from the news media, radio and television. The day arrived for the egg drop, and we were going to have to make two flights because of so many parcels. We planned to have "bombs away" over a field west of the junior high school where the entire school population stood watching. When Roy and I were ready to take off with the first load. a photographer from a television station showed up, requesting to go with us to take pictures of the egg drop from the airplane. I asked him if he could wait for the second load, but he said he couldn't because of a deadline. I crowded him in the front seat with me, surrounded by dozens of packages.

As we taxied down the runway to take off, the photographer spoke up. "I am a minister. I only do this as a sideline."

"Praise the Lord," I answered. "You might like to know that you are riding with a couple of 'born again' children of God, Roy and I."

We started talking to him about the Lord Jesus, but he shut up like a clam, and we couldn't get an answer from him. Roy and I soon surmised that this man wanted us to know that he was somebody, a minister, but when he found out that he was with a couple of "Jesus Freaks," he didn't want any more to do with us. As I stopped the plane at the end of the runway to rev it up and check it out, I looked over to the minister and said, "I am real skeptical about taking anyone up in this plane who isn't saved, because I don't really know what is going to happen." He looked like he wanted to get out, but we took him up anyway.

Help Me, God

After dropping off two passengers at the Traverse City Airport, it started to rain as I departed. Proceeding up the northern coastline to Charlevoix, the weather became much worse. I hated to have to turn around and go back through that weather, which was obviously getting worse behind me as well as in front of me. The clouds came down so low as to force me down to tree height. So I flew out over the bay where I only had to worry about the waves, which eliminated smokestacks, trees, buildings, towers and other obstacles that I no longer could see. I was able to look down and keep the shoreline in sight, even though I could not see ahead. I thought as I followed the shoreline I could tell when I came to the part of the shoreline opposite the Charlevoix Airport, if the visibility would increase to at least a mile or so.

As I came closer to that area, I prayed, "Lord, if you want me to land at Charlevoix, it will be necessary for you to increase the visibility."

About the time I thought I had gone past the Charlevoix Airport, the visibility increased and I looked inland and saw the Charlevoix runway. I turned to the right and flew straight at the runway under a 100 foot cloud formation. The runway was only about two miles away. About halfway there, everything disappeared, and I found myself flying blind in clouds at an altitude that meant sure disaster.

I said, "Lord, I am going to give you 15 seconds to open a hole in the clouds, and if you don't, I am going to pull up through that soup, and my chances of ever finding my way down through this stuff without crashing is nil. I don't dare continue flying blind at this altitude."

I looked at my watch and at my instruments and started timing God's answer. When my watch ticked off 12 seconds, I saw a small hole in the clouds on my left, and through that hole I saw the end of the runway. I banked my plane sharply to the left, and scooted through that hole, landing downwind...but safely on the runway.

I taxied up to the terminal building, and getting out, I met two of my Christian friends waiting to pick me up. They both had sensed that I was in trouble and had been praying constantly to the Lord for my deliverance. Praise God for Christian friends, and for the closest friend of all, my pilot, Jesus!

No One Else Would Be This Crazy

My friend Brad had never been up in an airplane before, and he wasn't sure that he wanted to go now. We were making a trip to Central Michigan University at Mt. Pleasant,

Michigan. I was going to speak to some science classes and Brad was going to visit some of our hometown students. Brad had agreed to fly with me if the weather was good. The weather that morning was very marginal, in fact, was not good enough for VFR flying. I asked Brad to drive my car to Marshall and meet me at the airport, and I would make the ten minute flight with my plane. I would have some work done on my plane while we drove to Mt. Pleasant.

After meeting Brad at the Marshall airport, the weather looked better, and I persuaded Brad to fly to Mt. Pleasant from Marshall. I agreed to turn about and come back to Marshall if the weather turned worse ahead of us. We taxied out to runway niner which is due east, and I revved the motor and went through the check list. Brad was excited, very nervous and frightened. He asked, "Is the motor all warmed up? Do you have plenty of gas?" I assured him that everything was O.K. and we had both gas tanks practically full. He pointed at the compass which indicated E for east because the plane was facing due east and shouted, "That gas tank is empty." "You are a nut, Brad, that is the magnetic compass -- not a gas tank gauge," I informed him.

We were still about thirty miles from Mt. Pleasant when we flew into a hard rainstorm. Brad had asked me whether I had windshield wipers in case it started raining. I told him that I thought the propeller would blow the rain clear. In this rainstorm we could hardly see ahead, but could see the ground by looking straight down. Brad inquired, "Could you see another plane up here, Floyd, and not have a collision?" I tried to console Brad, "There wouldn't be anybody else crazy enough to be up in this stuff, Brad, so we don't have to worry about other planes."

By following the radio beam we were able to fly directly over the Mt. Pleasant airport which we could see as we looked down. Brad asked me, "Will you have any trouble landing on that rain-swept runway?" I assured him that I wouldn't have any difficulty. Then I remembered that I had never landed on a wet runway before. We landed without mishap. That night before we took off for Coldwater, I went up by myself first to check the weather and decided it was too bad to fly home. We stayed all night and flew back to Coldwater the next day.

Brad and I decided sometime later to go to Florida to tape interviews with the major league baseball players during spring training for the local radio station. We were based at the Detroit Tiger's training camp in Lakeland, Florida. However, Brad would not fly to Florida with me so I flew and he drove his car, and we met in Lakeland. One day we decided to go to Clearwater to see a game. I talked Brad and his two teenage sons into flying as it would only take thirty minutes. It was a rough trip because of the high winds. Brad and one of his sons were frightened the entire trip. As we landed, Brad looked at his watch and said, "Twenty-eight minutes of torture and I am taking the bus back." And his one son said, "Me, too."

I spent most of the game talking Brad into flying back with us. I told him that the wind would go down and we would have a real smooth trip back. He and his son finally consented. It was smooth flying back, so Brad and his son worried about running into jets and having a fatal collision. I said, "Brad, those jets don't want to hit us any more than we want to hit them. Those pilots know what they are doing, even if you think I don't."

I had the pleasure and opportunity of performing the marriage ceremony when Brad married his second wife. As I counseled with them before the marriage they both professed Jesus, and are now living a happy, fruitful life.

2

THE TIME IS SHORT

A Merciful God

Pete and Sally had been invited, and had decided to attend a home Bible study one night when I was teaching in Coldwater, Michigan. Pete sat on my left; Sally across the room. Sally had been married before and had one child, but she and Pete planned to get married in a few months. Out of the dozen people at the study, I sensed that Pete and Sally wished that they had not come. You could tell that both of them seemed uncomfortable while we read and discussed the Scriptures and Jesus. In fact, I am sure both of them would have walked out if they had had the courage. I tried to relieve the pressure by making friends, and not pushing the scriptures at them. After this one Bible study experience, they never came back.

On March 18, 1974, I was traveling in northern Michigan for special meetings and personal witnessing. That night I called home. My wife told me something had happened to Pete and Sally. They had been looking for a house to buy since their marriage was approaching. A real estate lady showed them a home that was unoccupied. The lights were shut off and apparently one of the three lit a match. The house, filled with leaking propane gas, exploded in flame. Pete and Sally were burned on 95 per cent of their bodies and were rushed to the burn center at St. Joseph Hospital in Ann Arbor, Michigan.

When I arrived home a week later, they both had asked to see me. I flew to Ann Arbor and took a taxi to the hospital. To prevent infecting them, a nurse dressed me in a rubber hat, a long apron, a mask, rubber covers over my shoes, and rubber gloves.

I was taken to Pete's bedside first. The initial sight of Pete was a shock, even though I've seen many bad accidents. His body was completely covered with blood-soaked bandages, except for his charred cheeks and his eyes. Several tubes were assisting his body functions. Coughing and choking, he could not talk.

I asked, "Pete, do you know that I am Coach Eby?"

He acknowledged with his eyes and nodded his head slightly. In spite of his pain and injury, his mind was clear. He could understand what I was saying.

"Pete," I asked. "Do you want me to talk to you about Jesus?" I then slowly and carefully told Pete of God's Plan for his life. As I read each verse, I explained how it applied to him in joining the Family of God. He accepted the explanation of each verse with a slight nod and by the look in his eyes. As I summarized the three steps of joining the Family of God there was no doubt he understood. I knew he had accepted Jesus as his Savior and had received the Holy Spirit into his charred body. I asked if he wanted me to pray for him and Sally, and he vigorously indicated he did. We both went to the Throne of Grace, praising God for Pete's decision.

As I started to leave, Pete made some funny noises, trying to tell me something. I called a doctor over and he put an ear down to Pete's mouth, but he couldn't decipher it either. Finally a nurse unhooked a tube temporarily and put her ear down to his mouth. She looked up and said Pete wanted to ask if I would marry him and Sally when they were better. I told him I certainly would under God, and he seemed to have complete peace.

After a long wait, I was taken to see Sally. She seemed to be even worse off than Pete, but I talked to her and found her mind was also clear and she could understand me. As I started to explain God's Plan for her life, two nurses and a doctor continued to work on Sally.

I stepped back and asked, "Do you wish me to wait until you are through?"

"No," the doctor replied, "you go right ahead and say what you have to say. We have to work constantly on this girl."

So I explained to Sally as I had to her fiance how she could enter the Family of God. She also clearly accepted each step and verse. Eager to know how, she accepted without hesitation or reluctance. As I talked to Sally, I took the opportunity to witness at the same time to the doctor and nurses. After praying with Sally, once again thanking Jesus for His compassion and Sally's decision, I went out into the hall. The doctor and both nurses came out and talked with me about faith in God.

Six weeks later, Sally went home to be with her Lord and Saviour. Two weeks later Pete joined her and his precious Saviour.

People ask, "What kind of loving God is that, to allow two young people to burn to death?" I say that it is a merciful God that allowed Pete and Sally time on earth to get right with their Jesus, before passing into Eternity.

Now they have no more pain, and can enjoy the free gift of Eternal Life, the reward of their decision to accept Jesus Christ our Lord!

God has also used this tragic happening to cause several people from both families to come in to the Family of God. Believers also have come closer to the Lord because of this accident, including the author of this book. Praise God! He works out all things for the good of those who love Him.

Listen To God

One night a friend called and asked, "Do you remember

Dave?"

Sure, I remembered Dave. He was a former band instructor, and a real top-notch one at a school where I used to teach. Dave had changed jobs, and was now in charge of all television programs and facilities at a vocational school. According to my friend, Dave's wife had left him, taking his two sons with her, and he was really "shook up" about it. My friend thought I should go over and talk to him, and I told him I would try to do just that.

After hanging up the phone, I sat down in a chair in front of the television set, picked up the daily paper, and started to read. I had trouble concentrating on my reading, even though I had already made up my mind that I would try to look Dave up in the next two or three weeks. As I continued to attempt to read the paper, something was bothering me. Feeling it was the Lord, I spoke to Him.

"Lord, if you expect me to go over there tonight, forget it, you must know how tired I am and that I need some rest and relaxation. After all, I've had a tough day."

So I tried to continue my reading. But I had no rest or concentration.

I jumped out of my chair and threw the paper into the chair in disgust.

"O.K. Lord. If that is really what you want, I will go now."

I dressed and jumped into my car and headed for Dave's house.

Arriving there, I found Dave by himself. He was distraught. His depression was so great, I silently wondered if he might commit suicide. However, as I talked to him he didn't mention this possibility. In working with people and their problems, I have found that those who talk suicide usually do not commit the act, but the people who commit the act, do not talk about it.

I presented Dave with a couple of Bibles as gifts and told him how the Lord had changed my life, and had given me a happy and fruitful life in Jesus. Also I told him how he could have this same exciting life, with or without his mate.

Some ninety minutes later, Dave professed his faith in

THE TIME IS SHORT / 37

Jesus, and joined the Family of God.

Dave read and studied the Bible for hours and hours, and attended a weekly Bible study. The power of God's precious Word became a reality in Dave's life. Dave changed from the most depressed man in the city to one of the happiest. He not only started attending church regularly, but became the choir director, using his God-given talent to the glory of His Saviour.

One night, at one of the weekly Bible studies, before he closed in prayer, Dave made the following statement, "I love the Word of God, and I love this small group. Both have meant so much to me, and have helped me have a happy life; and if that man over there," he pointed directly at me, "had not come over to see me that night, I would not have been alive the next day."

I really shudder to think how close I came to turning God and Dave down that night, just because I didn't want to inconvenience myself.

I was only selfishly thinking of my own comfort and desires. When God speaks, we need to listen and obey. Dave has now married a fine Christian lady, and is living a happy life in Jesus.

Jesus Leading

I was conducting a Bible study in a mobile home from 11:00 p.m. to midnight. Barry, the owner of the mobile home, brought in two new girls for the first time, a sophomore and a senior in high school. When new people come to my Bible studies, I usually proceed with my lesson as previously planned. Then sometime within the next two or three weeks, I see if God will open the door where I can sit down with them, talk with them about their personal salvation, and how they can receive it.

However, this night God seemed to be leading differently. I spoke to the group. "If it is all right with the rest of you, I am going to discard my prepared lesson tonight. I am going to spend the hour telling these two young ladies about God's wonderful Plan for their lives. I want to tell Darlene and Linda, according to the Scriptures, how they can join the Family of God; and what an exciting adventure and wonderful time is waiting for them as soon as they join up, get close to God and put Him first in their lives. This is just too good to keep from them. Is that all right with the rest of you?" "Yeh, that's all right," they replied. So I spent the hour telling Darlene and Linda about Jesus, and the necessary steps, according to the Scriptures, that each had to take in order to join this Family of God and become our Sisters in Christ. Both girls professed Jesus as Saviour.

I had never met either one of these girls before this night. The next time I saw Linda, the senior, was two weeks later in her casket. She had drowned. I went to the funeral home on Friday night, because I could not attend the funeral services on Saturday.

I asked for Linda's father. We went into a room by ourselves.

"Sir, I am Coach Eby. I want to tell you what happened to your daughter, Linda, two weeks ago in a mobile home Bible study."

He exploded. "If you want to tell me about that wonderful, loving, compassionate, powerful God; forget it. I don't think much of a God who would let my daughter drown in the prime of her life!"

"Sir, I want you to know that I had the privilege of opening up God's precious Word that night, and telling your daughter about God's wonderful Plan for her life. According to the Scriptures, Linda accepted Christ that night as Saviour and joined the Family of God. She is now safe, home in the arms of Jesus according to God's promises. And sir, I want to tell you that Linda is much better off right now than you or I."

I started to leave and he replied, "I will tell you one thing, she sure was reading those two Bibles each day that you had given her."

Once again, I was happy that I had sought and followed God's nudge that night to junk my prepared lesson, and tell Linda how to accept God's gift of salvation. I would not have wanted to attend her funeral knowing that she had gone into a Christless Eternity, because I had not followed God's leading.

I flew to Washington, D.C. on the Lord's business. A week later, I arrived home and attended church on that Sunday night. After the service, I went through my week's mail. I received a letter from a lady in Bangor, Michigan. She wrote, "Sir, I don't know you, and you don't know me, but I am Linda's grandmother. Three days before she drowned, Linda visited me, and she told me about you. She gave me your name and address. Linda told me about the mobile home Bible study that you conducted at midnight, and how you had told her about Jesus, and how she had accepted Christ and joined the Family of God. I want you to know that she opened up the Bible, and told me about Jesus."

A few months later, I was giving this same testimony on television. Afterwards, one of the cameramen, whom I didn't know, came up to me and said, "Praise the Lord."

"Sure," I responded, "Praise the Lord. What are you praising Him about today?"

"I have only been saved for one year," he said. I sat right in back of Linda in a class in high school. After she drowned, I felt so bad that I had not talked to her about Jesus. So I am praising the Lord for saving her anyway."

God does work in marvelous ways, doesn't He?

Just In Time

One day I was making some calls in a rural area. I had talked to a young couple about Jesus, and they had professed salvation, but I was unable to get them interested in a Bible study or regular fellowship. I had always felt compassion for this young man, because he was in my class as a ninth grader, and was a very promising athlete when I was coaching sports at this same school. However, due to a malignant tumor, he had to drop athletics and school, but miraculously recovered some years later.

The day I was making calls, I debated whether to stop and see Sam or not. It would be a couple miles out of my way, and

I reasoned that he probably would not be home, anyway. However, I turned my car and went to Sam's mobile home and found him there by himself. I talked to him about Jesus and the necessity of being sure that he had had a personal encounter with Jesus. He sealed the decision that day. The next day, Sam was killed in an automobile accident, and went home to be with his Lord and Saviour. Praise God for His timing!

The Door Is Shut

Matthew 25:10 states that those who were ready went in with Him to the marriage feast, and the door was shut. As I fly my plane out of Detroit on a clear night, I can see lights for miles and miles; even those of Toledo, Monroe, Port Huron, Pontiac, all the suburbs of Detroit, and that great city of Detroit itself. Almost one-half of the population of Michigan is concentrated in Wayne County, and I can see literally millions of lights representing millions of people. I never fly over this area at night without thinking of these millions of people who are headed for a Christless Eternity, because they do not know Jesus Christ as their personal Saviour. I also realize that the door is being shut on hundreds of them each week as they die of illness, accidents, homicides, suicides, and old age without Christ. Oh, how important it is that we be about the Lord's business of telling others before the door is shut on many more.

Yes, Brethren, the time is very, very short!

Finally, Brethren, whatsoever things are true, whatsoever things are honest, whatsoever things are just, whatsoever things are pure, whatsoever things are lovely, whatsoever things are of good report; if there be any virtue, and if there be any praise, think on these things.
Philippians 4:8

A WONDERFUL WAY OF LIFE

My Own Testimony

I was raised on a farm by my Christian parents, Jesse and Marcia Eby, along with two brothers and a sister. Materially, we were a poor family, and I resented this poverty and the fact that I had to go without many things my friends had. Although my parents were Christians, I was not, and vowed that I was going to be concerned about obtaining desirable things for myself. I wanted to be a coach and teacher, a sports announcer, a pilot, and to make money.

I praise God that I lived in a country where a nobody like me could come off a farm and in a few short years obtain all the goals I desired. However, for many years I lacked the one really important ingredient for complete happiness; *a personal encounter with the Lord Jesus!*

Although I had heard hundreds of sermons, Sunday school lessons, etc., I had never really joined the Family of God. My mother was sick for ten years when I was a small boy, and a young teenager. I was not a Christian, but I prayed on my knees each night that God would make my mother well. He never did, and I hated God for that! My mother passed away when I was a freshman at college. For many years, my interest was in playing and coaching sports, teaching, airplanes, making money, and becoming prominent and popular. I went to church, taught Sunday school classes, but wasn't too interested in spiritual things. I thought I was a Christian headed toward Heaven because of the good life I was living, in serving my community and helping young people.

During World War II, while a Communication Officer overseas on a Destroyer Escort, I started reading the Bible and found that I was a lost sinner in spite of my goodness, and I knew that I was outside the protection of God. However, in attempting to make the Bible practical, and to prove it, I became a confused young man. Finally, one day I decided to either become an atheist, and throw out all this religious nonsense, or accept God for what He says He is! Right then, I decided to accept each word of God as truth by faith that God is no liar, and I have not been confused since.

However, for years I grew very slowly spiritually, as I did not consistently do the things needed to grow close to God. I read the Bible occasionally, went to church, but did not discipline myself to be consistent in Bible reading, praying, being with other Christians, and serving Jesus.

I was making more money than ever before. One day my Lord shook me up: Galatians 6:7 "Be not deceived, God is not mocked; for whatsoever a man soweth, that shall he also reap." I lost $40,000.00 in two business deals within three days, and immediately I asked my Lord, "Why me?" I reminded my Lord that I had been going to church regularly, teaching Sunday school class and giving thousands of dollars each year to my church and other missionaries.

My Lord answered me quickly, "Don't give me any more jazz about that money you are giving me. I want your dedication, time, and talent."

Right then, I surrendered my life, time, talent, and money

to my Saviour, and I have been richly blessed ever since. Each day with Jesus is sweeter than the day before!

Four Reasons Why I Believe and Know The Bible Is True

The following four reasons are why I believe and know the Bible is true. They really make sense to me now, and I pray they will also make sense to you, as belief in the Bible is the key to this wonderful way of life I am telling you about. *The first reason* I believe the Bible is the fulfilling of prophecies. You see, being a scientist, I believed in science, not the Bible. I now completely believe the Bible. Some top scientists are personal friends of mine, and they too at one time were atheists, believing only science and not the Bible. Dr. John Moore from Michigan State University was an avowed atheist until 1962. He believed in only science, and thought God, Jesus, and the Bible were nonsense as I did. In 1962, Dr. Moore became a Christian, and three years later in 1965, he was speaking to a group of men about the harmony of the Bible and science. By that time I believed the Bible, and I had taught science for many years, so I drove up to Michigan State University to hear him.

Dr. Moore used two illustrations that day that I still remember. "At one time," he said, "Science had established the fact that there were just 1,054 stars in the Universe." May I ask you readers if you ever tried counting the stars on a clear night? Well, I have, and I have found out that when you get up to 15 or 20 stars, you become confused and mixed up and cannot keep track. I have also attempted to count them while in a planetarium where I used to teach about the sun, moon, and stars. It couldn't be done there either.

So, the scientists found they couldn't count the stars. They had collaborated and went to their experts; the books and charts...and established the scientific fact of 1,054 stars in the Universe, no more and no less. But while we scientists had established this fact, God's Word had already recorded in Genesis 15:5 that God compared the number of stars with the seed of people, or millions of people. Also, in Hebrew 11:12,

God compared the number of stars with the grains of sand at the seashore. Did you ever try to count the grains of sand when you were swimming on a sandy beach?

You see, friends, when science had established the fact of 1,054 stars, God's Word had already recorded that the stars were too numerous to be counted, and now science agrees with the Bible on this.

Dr. Moore also stated that at one time, science had established the fact that the earth was hung in place by cables. Of course, we laugh at that now, because we know that we place things in orbit and around and around they go with nothing attached thereto. Science at that time knew about gravity, but not about space, so science just knew that the earth had to be hooked to something, or it would fall out of space. After talking with the experts -- checking their books and charts -- we scientists decided that it was a fact that the Earth was hung in space by cables.

However, as we go to Job 26:7 we read that God hangeth the earth up on nothing. God's Word is continuing to prove scientific facts as wrong, and the only time that the Bible and science disagrees is when science is wrong! Praise God!

The second reason I believe the Bible, and know that it is true, is because it changes people's lives.

Yes, I was one of those people who used to ridicule matured Christians.

"Look at that religious nut. He has gone nuts on religion. He is a fanatic. He is way out in left field. They ought to lock him up and throw away the key. Man -- is he gone!" I used to say.

However, no matter how much I ridiculed the Christians, in my own mind, I had to admit that something was changing their lives, even though the way He was changing them was distasteful to me at the time. Then when God came in and changed my life and thousands of my friends' lives, I knew it was for real. So it makes sense that the Bible is true if it has the power to change lives.

The third reason I believe the Bible, and know that it is true, is because God is no liar. When I was over seas I had to make a decision, as I asked myself this question. "Is God the greatest liar ever created, the greatest phony ever produced, the greatest fake ever brought about -- or does He tell the truth and is He what He claims He is?"

You see God is not like Floyd Eby, as I tell the truth most of the time and sometimes I lie. But God is either what He claims He is, or He is the greatest liar ever created.

I decided right then and there that *God is no liar.* From the point of starting, I now could make a simple scientific deduction. If God is no liar, then He tells the truth. If He tells the truth, then God said He wrote the Bible, then it has to all be true, because God only tells the truth. I believe that there can be a few errors in some translations, but I know there is not one error in the original writings, as God wrote it.

In II Peter 1:20-21 we read, "Knowing this first, that no prophecy of the scripture is of any private interpretation. For the prophecy came not at any time by the will of man, but holy men of God spoke as they were moved by the Holy Spirit." If you wished to write a book and asked me to type as you dictated it to me, and I typed every word just as you told it to me, who would be the author of the book, you or me? You, of course. I was only the typist. You were the author and you understood everything that you wrote even though someone else might read your book and misunderstand some parts of it.

I believe this is the way that God's Book was written. God told these Holy Men of God just what to put down. In other words, these Holy Men of God -- John, Paul, Peter and all the others had no choice but to write down exactly what God spoke to them through His Holy Spirit.

I used to say that I thought parts of the Bible were true, but other parts were not or could not be. However, this same God who cannot lie and wrote the Bible states in II Timothy 3:16, "All scripture is given by inspiration of God, and is profitable for doctrine, for reproof, for correction, for instruction in righteousness." God said, "I wrote it all." The Bible in the original writings has to be true, or none of it is true, because God wrote all of it.

The key to our salvation, our faith, our blessings, and all of

God's Promises, are wrapped up in the *fact* that God is no liar. Therefore He tells the truth. Therefore He wrote the Bible. Therefore the Bible has to be true, and we can only rely on His Word for salvation, faith, blessings, and all of God's promises.

The fourth reason I believe the Bible and know that it is true, is that I accept by faith that which I cannot understand.

As you read this, I know many of you are saying to yourselves, "Not me, I want everything proven to me." I could prove everything in the Bible to you if only I could place myself on the same intellectual level as God Almighty who wrote the Book. Of course, this is impossible, so I need to accept the parts of the Bible I cannot understand by Faith, because God said it. I personally fought this concept for years. I am a scientist, a coach, and a teacher, and I wanted all things proven to me as facts. As I diagrammed new football plays, and every man did his job and blocked his man, we would run for a touchdown every play. But we seldom did, because someone was "goofing off," and would miss his man. But I realize that we use faith in our daily living.

One morning one of my high school students came to me in the hall. "Coach Eby, I have some questions to ask you," she said.

"Wait until you come to my first class, Sally," I replied, "and we will discuss your questions then."

When the class started, and I gave the students a reading assignment, I took Sally into my adjacent office, and asked her what I could do to help her. She handed me a sheet of questions, and I quickly looked at them and found the questions to be all anti-God and anti-Christian.

"Did you make up these questions, Sally?"

"No," came the answer, "I got them from my boyfriend at the University."

I thought to myself, this is about "par" for the course.

"This is Friday," I said. "Let me take your questions home over the weekend, and I will look up the answers in God's Word."

The next Monday morning in the hallway, Sally asked if I had the answers to her questions, and I told her I would see her in class. Once again I took her to my office.

"Yes, Sally," I said. "I have some answers to your questions, but you are not going to be satisfied with them."

"Why not?" She asked.

"Because you don't accept the Bible as true and God's Word."

I took the Bible from my desk and held it up. "We must accept the parts of the Bible we can't understand by faith, because God said it."

Sally struck the desk with her fist, and indignantly replied, "You are just like the rest of them. I thought you could help me but you're just like the others, expecting me to accept the Bible on blind faith. I just won't do that because I am not that type of person."

"I am sorry, Sally, that you don't live with your mother." I mentioned.

"But I do," she said.

"No, you don't," I replied.

"Yes I do."

"No you don't."

"Yes, I do. You know I do, Coach. You have been to my home and I have introduced you to my mother."

"I regret to inform you, Sally, that is not your real mother. I think you got mixed up in the hospital and were sent to the wrong home."

"I know better than that," Sally protested.

"How do you know, Sally? Did you ever have a blood test? Even that would not prove it for sure."

By now Sally was somewhat confused, and I said to her, "Sure, Sally, you know she is your mother and I know she is your mother, but only through faith that we accept."

Sally saw the point.

Once in a while my teenage daughter would act nasty at home, and sometimes I would say to her, "You know, you are no daughter of mine. My daughter would not act like that. You must have been mixed up in the hospital, and sent to the wrong home." Her mother would answer, "She acts just like her dad."

If I asked you readers who the first President of the United States was, most of you would tell me, George Washington. I buy that. In fact, if someone today was able to prove to me that George Washington wasn't the first President of the United States, I would be disturbed, because all my life I have known that Washington was the first President. I read it in history books. I would like to ask you the question, "Does it make sense to believe without a shadow of a doubt, a history book written by men and women, accepting George Washington as the first President of the United States and many other historical events, and not believe a book (the Bible) written by God?" I am sure your answer is, that if we are to accept history books by faith, we must accept the Bible by Faith!

In summary, I believe that the Bible is true, because of the fulfilling of prophecies; because it changes peoples' lives; because God is no liar, and He said He wrote the Bible, and because I accept those parts of the Bible I cannot understand by faith because God said it.

This makes sense to me and I am sure it does to you. If it does make sense to you, then the scriptures can show you as they showed me, the way to join the Family of God.

God Shows The Way

Since we now believe and know that the Bible is true, God will show us through four verses of scripture how to join the Family of God. The first verse is Romans 3:23 "For all have sinned, and come short of the glory of God." For many years I have thought this verse included everyone except Floyd Eby, but one day I realized that the "all" in the English language means everybody but Jesus, and that includes *all* evangelists, *all* preachers, *all* men, *all* women, *all* children, and most of all, it included me. You see, I don't know one bad thing about you and you don't know anything bad about me, because we don't know each other. But as you read this book, you know that Floyd Eby does some wrong. You know that much without even knowing me, because God says in this verse that

A WONDERFUL WAY OF LIFE / 49

all do wrong, and that not only has to include me, but you, too. Therefore, you and I are in the same boat. We both do wrong and we need help. In fact, we need the Saviour. Another important truth of this verse is that it takes any right away from me to criticize your way of living. If I criticize the things you do, then I am judging you for the same things I do. You might wonder if I do the same wrong things you do. Maybe not, but God says I do wrong, and wrong is wrong. I have all I can do to keep my relationship between me and Jesus in proper condition.

The second verse is Romans 6:23 "For the wages of sin is death, but the gift of God is eternal life through Jesus Christ our Lord." Sometimes, we get all mixed up in terminology. You've heard of people becoming Christians, having eternal life, everlasting life, going to Heaven, being born again, being saved, and joining the Family of God. I have heard people say that they are one of the above, but not another, and so on. But according to the Scriptures, the terms all mean the same thing. The term I like to use is that when I took the necessary steps by faith in Jesus, I joined the Family of God. This makes all Christians brothers and sisters in Christ.

In order to receive a gift, three facts have to be present. First, the gift has to be free. Second, the giver has to be willing to give it. And third, the recipient has to be willing to receive it. It cannot be a gift unless all of these facts are present.

If I told you I was going to give you a Bible, but I never did, it would never become a gift. If I charged you even ten cents for it, it would not be a gift because you paid for it. Therefore, it wasn't free. On the other hand, I could be willing to give you this Bible free, and you could say, "Take your Bible, Eby, and keep it. I don't want it." It would never become a gift because you had exercised your right to reject it.

God has a free gift that He wants to give every one of us, but we have the right to accept it or reject it. If we don't accept it, then we reject it. Even though God wants all of us to have it, He will not force it on us, because He has given each of us a free choice.

You see, friends, we have a wonderful God. He has so set

up His plan for our lives that no one has to go to Heaven if he doesn't want to. Isn't that wonderful? Because God gave Floyd Eby a choice, and I rejected it for many years, I should not force my beliefs on anyone else who isn't willing to read or listen. In fact, I always tell people that as I am talking to them about Jesus, if they don't want to hear it, just say so, and I will turn off. This is God's Way.

The third verse is John 1:12...''But as many as received Him, to them gave He power to become the children of God, even to them that believe on His Name.'' We have our choice, but if we do accept His gift, we immediately become a child of God. I was brought up in a poor family on a farm in poverty conditions. What money we had, most of it had to go for my mother's doctor and hospital bills. I could not have the things that my friends had. I couldn't even have a used bicycle, much less a car. I had to work when the other boys could play ball. I resented this poverty, and vowed I was going to do something about it. You see, my mother and father loved me, but they were limited in what they could do for me because of the lack of material substance. I sometimes wished that I had been born to a different Mom and Dad, so I could have the things some of my friends had. I realize now how foolish it was for my childish mind to think this way, but you see, my parents had limitations. But when I joined the Family of God, God became my Heavenly Father, and He has no limitations like my earthly Mom and Dad had. My Heavenly Father owns the whole world and everything in it, and there is nothing that He cannot do. He can give me health or He can take it away from me. He has done both in my lifetime. He can give me wealth or He can take it away from me. He has done both in my lifetime. He can keep my plane aloft, or let it crash, and Praise God, He has done only one so far. It was, and still is, a real thrill to join a family with a father for whom all things are possible.

The fourth verse is Revelation 3:20...''Behold, I stand at the door, and knock, if any man hear my voice, and open the door, I will come in to him, and will sup with him, and he with me.'' Since we know that God wrote the Bible, and that Jesus was

God when He was on the earth, then we know as we read the verse Revelation 3:20, it is actually Jesus speaking to you and me. As I talk with people all over the United States, I find the great "hang-up" on Christianity is all the Do's and Don'ts that churches, ministers, and other Christians throw at people. But I find that God and His Word do not do this. There is absolutely nothing we have to do to acquire salvation. When Jesus spoke to me overseas he didn't say, "Floyd, I stand at the door and knock. If you quit cheating on your income tax, quit smoking, quit drinking, quit using drugs, quit swearing, quit running around on your wife, quit gambling, quit dancing, and hear my voice and invite me in, I will come in." No, Jesus didn't put *any* conditions to my accepting Him as my Saviour and joining the Family of God, except to invite Him into my life, and believe and have faith that He will come in. All Jesus said was, "Floyd, I stand at the door and knock, and if you hear my voice and invite me in, I will come in, and you will become my child." Jesus is no liar. He will do just that. Jesus is not talking about the front doors of our houses, but about our bodies. He says that He is ready at any time to send His Holy Spirit into our bodies and lives, and make us children of God, if we just invite Him in and mean it!

My Decision to Receive Christ As My Saviour

Confessing to God that I am a sinner, believing that the Lord Jesus Christ died for my sins on the cross, and was raised for my justification, I do now receive and confess Him as my personal Saviour.

When I was overseas, in the United States Navy, at the age of 26, I took the three necessary steps, according to the Scriptures, and joined the Family of God. To take *Step One*: I had to promise God that when He told me I had done wrong, I would come to Him, and be truly sorry and ask for His forgiveness, and He would forgive me. Please notice only God can tell me what I am doing wrong. He has the only right to judge me. You have no right because you are a sinner also.

Also, please notice that I do not have to tell any evangelist, minister, friend, relative, counselor, psychiatrist, or even my wife. I only have to tell God, and He already knows, so that is no big deal, and did not present a problem to me. I sincerely promised God that I would do this.

Step Two: I have to believe that Jesus, who is God upon the earth, died on the cross for your sins and my sins. Now, I don't understand this at all, but there is one part of it that I can understand, and that is how Jesus can love you and me enough to give up His life for us, if that is the way He wants to do it. I am sure if you have a son or daughter, and they were out in the street, and a huge truck was going to run over them, you would rush out to the street, and push them out of the way of the truck - even though it meant losing your own life. You would say, "Yes, I would do that because of my love for my children." However, I could offer you 10 million dollars to lay down in front of a large truck and be squashed to death, and you would turn the proposition down. You wouldn't sacrifice your life for money but you would for love. I would do the same for my daughters.

Now, if this is true of you and me, then we have to admit if we can love that much, then we know that Jesus, who is Divine, is capable of much greater love than you or I. So, certainly we can understand how He can love us enough to give up His life for us if that is the way He wants it.

I still don't understand how being nailed to the cross, crucified, and the shedding of His blood paid for my sins. But I don't have to understand, because He stated in the Bible that He wrote, that is the way He did it, and remember God is no liar!

Step Three: I have to believe that after Jesus was crucified and died on the cross, He was taken down and put in a tomb. Three days later He arose from the dead. Now, I don't understand how God did this, but I do know that God states four times in the Old Testament and four times in the New Testament in different words but all meaning the same thing: *that with God all things are possible* -- and God is no liar. God wrote the Bible, and He said He arose from the dead, and so I believe it.

Salvation is simple, sure, and complete. We must promise God that we will be truly sorry for our sins, we must believe that Jesus died on the cross for our sins, and that three days later Jesus arose from the dead for our justification. If we really mean it when we say to Jesus that we do believe, accept, and actually receive these three steps into our being by faith, then according to the scriptures, you and I are truly children of God and have joined the Family of God. We are truly brothers and sisters in Christ.

Congratulations on the greatest, most profitable, and wonderful decision you have ever made. God loves you and me, and I love you sister and brother!

*"Ye are my friends, if ye
do whatsoever I command you."*
John 15:14

4

MAKING FRIENDS WITH JESUS

Since we now have joined the Family of God, what a wonderful, exciting, and tremendous adventure we have waiting for us.

God's Word is full of promises which He is anxiously waiting to fulfill for each one of His children. We now can expect to look forward to a life filled with exciting and wonderful events each and every day. We can look forward with anticipation to every new day, which can, and will be better than the day before.

I personally have been endowed with all of the secular things of this world -- we all seek -- even before I joined the Family of God. I was fortunate to have an excellent job in a wonderful profession, a wonderful family, much publicity, community status, a beautiful home, new cars, my own plane, many friends, successful businesses, money, state basketball championships, football and baseball championships, and many other honors during my short lifetime.

However, even though many of these accomplishments were exciting and thrilling, each one eventually became routine.

The new cars were great. But I didn't wash them much

after the first month, and they soon faded into routine transportation.

The glow of athletic championships soon grew dim, and faded into just pleasant memories.

The making of money became an obsession that didn't leave time for the better things of life. The beautiful new home and swimming pool were wonderful, but soon became commonplace.

Becoming a successful business executive was a real boost to my ego, but presented many problems in living a happy, fruitful life. The publicity and honors made me feel important, but all were soon forgotten. When I first flew my own plane all by myself, I thought this was it. The ultimate. But it, too, became just a good way to travel.

All of the above became routine until I joined the Family of God, and I started using the above accomplishments to serve my Saviour. The only part of my life that never becomes routine is my personal relationship with the Lord Jesus. As I know Him better and better, every day gets better and better, and my relationship with Jesus is sweeter each and every day.

After we join the Family of God, Jesus only asks us to become His close friend. Another way of putting it is to grow spiritually, get closer to God, get to know Him better and better, putting God first, or increasing our faith. Jesus doesn't give us do's and don'ts. He just tells us how to become His close friend, and He will take care of everything else.

Each child of God is handled as a special case by Jesus. Our own relationship with Jesus has nothing to do with anybody else, because He holds us responsible according to our spiritual age.

Let's say you are one-year-old, and you are walking. You trip over your mom's best lamp and smash it. Your mother doesn't beat the tar out of you, because you are not old enough to know better. If you did it a few years later on purpose, she would let you know in no uncertain terms that it was wrong. You see, friends, we hold our children responsible according to their chronological age, and the law also holds us responsible to some degree according to our age. But God holds us responsible according to our spiritual age, and all of us may be at different spiritual ages or levels. How do I know this? Because there are things I could do a couple of years ago that were all right between me and my Saviour that I cannot do now, because I am now closer to God, and older spiritually.

Many times when dope addicts and alcoholics join the Family of God, the first question they ask is, "Do I have to give up my dope and alcohol now?" I always reply, "You don't have to give up anything." "What did you say?" they will ask. "I said, you don't have to give up anything. Just make friends with Jesus. He will change your life at the accepted time, and you don't have to give up anything. He will take it away from you and make it a blessing. I know it, because that is how He is changing my life."

After I became a Christian, I still played poker with my coaching friends. It was a small friendly game where you lose or win five or ten dollars during the evening. At the time it wasn't wrong between me and my Jesus to play poker, as He didn't speak to me about it. However, as I grew spiritually, Jesus started speaking to me. He let me know that it wasn't a very good example to my coaching friends, and might instead be a stumbling block to their own personal encounter with Jesus.

I spoke back to the Lord, "Lord, I love to play poker, and I am not going to give it up."

As I continued to play each week, my leadings from the Lord became stronger. I finally rationalized that playing poker wasn't bad. It was winning that was bad. I decided I would continue to play poker, but I would make sure that I would not win. However, I didn't want to lose very much so I played it close to my belt, and tried to lose only a dollar or so.

I played three more weeks and I won each time. The only times I had ever been a consistent winner. I still refused to stop playing. I rationalized that playing poker wasn't bad, and winning wasn't bad, but taking the winnings home was bad. So when I would leave the game about midnight, I would take my winnings, put them in the next pot and tell my friends to play for them.

"Take your filthy earnings home Eby. We don't want your filthy money. Take it, and forget it," they would remark sarcastically.

I would tell them I didn't want their money, and I would leave. After a couple of weeks of this, on my way home I thought...here I am fighting God on this, and even making my best friends mad at me, and that was the last of my poker playing. You see, I really didn't give it up, but God took it away from me, and made it a real blessing. I no longer had God on my back, or my friends mad at me, and my wife was real happy, and I felt good, and what a blessing it was to please Jesus. However, I am not saying it is wrong for other Christians if you gamble. It is wrong for a Christian to do anything that is displeasing to Jesus, and He will let you know when you displease Him, and this will continually change as we grow spiritually.

The important question is how to grow spiritually -- how to know Him better and better -- how to get closer to God -- how to put God first -- how to increase our faith -- how to become a real close friend of Jesus?

When I first meet someone, I may decide that I really like this guy, and I want to become a real close friend of his. This would be impossible if I decided that I never wanted to see him again, never wrote to him, never telephoned him, or visited him. We would feel that such actions would be stupid, if we were really trying to be close friends. On the same basis, we cannot become a close friend of Jesus if we refuse to read about Him in His Bible, refuse to talk to Him in prayer, refuse to be with His people, and refuse to serve Him.

To become a close friend of Jesus, or to grow spiritually, or to get to know Him better, or to become closer to God, or to put Him first, or to increase our faith, we need to follow Jesus' commands to: *1. Read the Bible, 2. Talk with God, 3. Be with other Christians, 4. Serve Jesus.*

Read the Bible

"Till I come, give attendance to reading"
1 Timothy 4:13a

Study to show thyself approved unto God,
a workman that needeth not to be ashamed,
rightly dividing the word of truth.''
2 Timothy 2:15

Many people after they have joined the Family of God (I have encouraged them to read the Bible) have come back and told me they were having trouble understanding it. I answer, "Hallelujah! Join the crowd. There are many things in the Bible I can't understand either. But God doesn't tell me that I must understand it; just that I must read or hear it."

If we do read or hear it, our Lord will reveal truths to us as we are ready for these truths, and He will bless our lives. However, if we refuse to read or hear it, He will not bless our lives by revealing truths from His Word. You and I could read the same chapter at the same time, and perhaps God would reveal a truth to you and not to me, because you are ready for that truth, and I am not yet ready.

The things in the Bible that I can't understand do not bother me. It is the things that I do understand that I have trouble with, and many truths in the Bible are very simple and easy to understand. I therefore have no excuse before Jesus when I displease Him by not following His guidelines for my life.

The real fundamental, necessary truths needed for my salvation and spiritual growth were recorded in the Bible several times, in simple language, by several different Holy Men of God. Such fundamental beliefs as the Virgin Birth, the Crucifixion, the Resurrection, the Second Coming, and the belief that the Bible is God's Holy Inspired Word, are true and accurate because the original recordings were written by God Himself. Controversial doctrine is important to us and to our numerous different denominations. I am sure it pleases God for us to join with other Christians in a local fellowship of like faith and doctrine to promote the cause of Jesus. However, I believe there are only two groups when it comes to spirituality. Either we are believers or unbelievers. And if we are not believers, we are unbelievers. It is important that we love the

Lord Jesus Christ, and accept in faith the fundamental truths necessary to join the Family of God according to the Scriptures.

I believe much misunderstanding comes from the term "church" in the Bible. When God uses the term "church" in His Bible, I believe He is referring to a group of believers gathering for the purpose of worshipping our Lord. This can include all of the different denominations, organizations, church buildings, missionary groups, broadcasting, television, home Bible studies, prayer meetings, meetings in cars, planes, or on the job. I don't believe our Lord would just have us equate the biblical term church with a denominational organization and a church building.

We need to read the Bible daily, and the more we read, the more our Jesus will bless us with the truths needed to live a happy, fruitful life.

Talk With God

In the Bible, God commands us to talk or pray to Him. I Timothy 2:8 "I will, therefore, that men pray everywhere, lifting up holy hands, without wrath and doubting." I Thessolonians 5:17 "Pray without ceasing." Acts 6:4 "But we will give ourselves continually to prayer, and to the ministry of the Word." Luke 18:1 "And He spoke a parable unto them to this end, that men ought always to pray, and not to faint."

To become a close friend to anyone, we need to talk and visit with them. The same is true if we become a close friend to Jesus; we need to talk and visit with Him, which many call prayer. We can talk to Him in public or in private, on our knees, or in any position, out loud or without utterance, at any time, and at any place, and about anything. To grow spiritually, we need to talk to God many times a day, and He will bless us for it!

Be With Other Christians

The Bible commands us to join in fellowship with believers, and people of like faith. Acts 2:42 "And they continued steadfastly in the apostles' doctrine and fellowship, and in breaking of bread, and in prayers." I John 1:3 "That which we have seen and heard declare we unto you, that ye also may have fellowship with us; and truly our fellowship is with the Father, and with his Son, Jesus Christ." I John 1:7 "But if we walk in the light, as He is in the light, we have fellowship one with another, and the blood of Jesus Christ, His Son, cleanseth us from all sin."

You would probably like to ask me if I ever associate with unbelievers? I certainly do. I have hundreds of coaching friends who believe just as I do, and I also have hundreds of friends who do not believe as I do. I have spent many a night talking basketball and football with coaching friends who were not Christians. I enjoyed these evenings very much, and there is not anything wrong with it. However, I have to admit that when I am with my unbelieving friends, nothing happens to get me closer to the Lord. In fact, I am drawn away from God. So you see, I need to spend the majority of my time with other people of like faith if I want to become a closer friend of Jesus, grow spiritually, get to know Him better, and better, or increase my faith. Christian people surrounding us with their presence, their compassion, concern, and love, will have a real influence on our spiritual growth. We have to be real strong spiritually, to keep an environment of unbelievers from dragging us away from our God.

What are some of the ways to obtain the needed Christian fellowship? Following is a suggested list: churches and other Christian Service Organizations, Christian friends, home Bible studies, Christian meetings and conferences, your own program of serving Jesus, Christian Schools, Christian parties, Christian excursions, the making of your own home into a place of Christian gatherings.

Serve Jesus

We are commanded by the Bible to obey and serve Jesus.

John 12:26 "If any man serve me, let him follow me; and where I am, there shall also my servant be; if any man serve me, him will my Father honour." Colossians 3:23,24 "And whatsoever ye do, do it heartily, as to the Lord, and not unto men." "Knowing that of the Lord ye shall receive the reward of the inheritance; for ye serve the Lord Christ." Ephesians 6:7 "With good will doing service, as to the Lord, and not to men."

When we start serving Jesus through His leading, we will really grow rapidly spiritually and get close to God. As we serve Him regularly, we will become His best friend, and He will shower us with abundant blessings. I don't know how God will have you serve Him, but I do know that if we grow spiritually, He will tell us how He would have us serve Him. I am sure God would have you serve Him differently than He has me. All I can do is tell you what doors of service He has opened for me: Giving messages about the Bible and my Lord at banquets, churches, schools, clubs, conferences and conventions; a witnessing and personal follow-up program; my church and many other service organizations; home Bible studies, television programs, jail ministry; counseling couples with marital trouble; counseling alcoholics, dope addicts, and law violators concerning help from God and the Bible; writing books, and through other avenues of service. God has opened so many doors that now it is thrilling to watch how He can guide me into new service by closing doors in present service. I can sincerely say that I have never been any happier than I am now when He has opened so many doors through which I can walk and receive real blessings. Praise His Holy Name!

Family Devotions

God will bless any family of believers who will designate a time each day and have a devotional period with all members of the family present. When you have it, during the day or night, will depend on the time necessary to have everyone present. Our devotional period is in the morning before breakfast, and consists of the reading of a portion of God's

Word, an illustration about the reading, prayer requests, and prayer. We know that forty per cent of all marriages today end up in divorce. But recent surveys taken of thousands of families who are Christians, go to church and other Christian meetings together, have daily devotions, read the Bible together daily, pray together daily, and take their problems to the Lord, indicate that only one out of 900 such marriages end up in divorce. I am sure you will agree that there is no marriage counselor, psychologist, psychiatrist, minister, or anyone else who can bring about such results. But God's precious Holy Inspired Word, the Bible, and the Holy Spirit can.

Things

Through my many years of working with all kinds of people with problems, I have found only one solution: The Bible and God. I have also found that 90 per cent of the people have "hang-ups" on Christianity, preachers, churches, Christians, and the Bible, because of all of the do's and don'ts that all the Christians have thrown at them. They have been told they would have to do this and not be able to do that. You must not smoke, drink, use dope, dance, play cards, wear mini-skirts, commit adultery, swear, steal, etc. I call this a list of "things."

I sincerely believe that no minister ever changed a person's life by preaching "things" from the pulpit. God's Word puts no restrictions or do's or don'ts in joining the Family of God. We need to preach and teach Jesus Christ and His Word in every temple and every house. As a person joins the Family of God and then grows spiritually under the preaching and teaching of Jesus Christ, then that person will have his life changed by the removal of the "things" by God at the accepted time.

Home Bible Studies

Acts 5:42 "And daily in the temple, and in every house, they ceased not to teach and preach Jesus Christ." I believe that we have attempted to spread the News of a Wonderful Saviour in the wrong way. We have established beautiful church buildings, hired articulate preachers, trained Sunday School teachers, organized our churches and Sunday Schools to the utmost, purchased buses, and have evangelistic meetings. We have then waited for the unsaved to come in, or have contests to draw them in or have calling programs to try and get them to the church. I am not saying that the above methods are wrong, but we have to admit the methods listed have not produced enough of the desired results.

Jesus traveled to where people were. He did not stay in one place and wait for people to show up. Jesus said, "Go, Ye." I believe we have to follow the example of Jesus; we need to go to where the people are. We need to go into homes; not to invite them to church, but to tell them about Jesus. We can "beat" a person over the head enough, and get him to church even two Sundays in a row. Then he stays home the third Sunday, and we have to start all over again.

Why would an unsaved person enjoy coming to church or to evangelistic meetings? Did you, before you were saved? We need to visit people in their own surroundings and explain salvation to them. Once they have joined the Family of God, and start growing in the Word, most of them will then want to come to church to be fed in the Word by our ministers, have fellowship with God's Children, and want to serve Jesus. We need to go to the homes, hippie communes, jails, hospitals, sanitariums, schools, civic clubs, and any other place that God opens up, and talk to people about Jesus and the Bible. We need to talk to people we work with, on breaks and at noon hours. We need to talk to them on the street, or during recreation whenever God opens a door.

People who will never attend a church will allow you to come to their home, if approached properly under God's Guidance, to talk with them about the Bible and Jesus and this new way of life. Neighbors will also come to your own home to read and discuss the Bible if you invite them. The home Bible study should be voluntary and permit free will in every aspect. Don't "bug" people if they miss; just keep inviting them. Be available, and pray for them, and let them know that you are praying for them. No one reads unless they choose to. Don't ask questions unless you are sure they are willing. Let them comment or give illustrations if they desire. Don't put anyone on the spot. Be simple in your teaching. Give them milk until they are ready for the meat. Teach the fundamental necessities of joining the Family of God and growing spiritually. Don't argue controversial doctrine. Emphasize the importance of loving the Lord Jesus, and do not push your own convictions down other people's throats.

God gave each one of us a choice, and we have no right to insist that others agree with us. The length of the Bible study will depend on the people involved, conditions, and God's leading. However, none of them should "drag." In one home I only spend from five to ten minutes, reading a few verses of scripture, make a few comments, ask for their prayer requests, and close in prayer. On the other hand, I have a home Bible study that lasts 90 minutes. Between these two extremes are many others with varying times.

Every new person should, within a few weeks, if not the same night, be taken through the scriptures, have God's Plan for his or her life explained, and be given the opportunity to make a decision. Be sure to make friends first. Don't talk "things" or problems; just talk Jesus and how to join His Family; how to get close to Him. Encourage people to get close to Him by reading the Bible, talking with Jesus, being with other Christians, and serving Jesus. All other "things" are up to God.

Discipline

We must discipline ourselves to grow spiritually and get close to God. It takes discipline on our part to do the things necessary to come close to God. It takes discipline to read the Bible daily, to pray daily, to be with Christians, and to serve Jesus. Many times there is other literature I would rather read than the Bible, but I know that the Bible only can give me a happy, fruitful life. So I must set a time aside daily to read the

Bible even if I would rather not. It takes discipline to pray daily especially when everything is going well. It is easy to spend time in prayer when we have problems like illness that we cannot handle. But how much time do we spend talking to God when we don't have any problems? God said, "Pray without ceasing." It takes discipline to be with other Christians. It might seem to be more fun to skip that Christian meeting and go to the ball game or go bowling, but our real happiness depends on fellowship of Christians to give us strength, and assurance for a really happy way of life. It takes discipline to serve Jesus when He calls us or leads us to serve Him. Sometimes, I would rather sit at home than to make a needed call. I am tired and weary, but fatigue is mainly of the mind, and the joy of serving Jesus will completely rest you. When we are completely exhausted over a period of time, God is able and will give us time to recover. Many times I have reached this point, and God has downed me and my plane with bad weather for a day or two, and I come back home completely rested. Our Wonderful Saviour knows and understands all of our needs.

5

"The fool hath said in his heart,
There is no God.
Psalms 53:1a

ATHEISM, A HOPELESS CONDITION

Even the Marines Need Help

I was showing an ex-Colonel of the United States Marines from Battle Creek, Michigan homes to buy as he was planning to move to Coldwater, and retire. Each time I showed him a home, and we would look at the basement while his wife remained upstairs, the Colonel would bring up the subject of religion. I found out that he knew many of the scriptures, and at one time had studied to be a minister. But while in school, the Colonel had decided that the Bible and God were all nonsense. He was now very antagonistic to anything that had to do with Christianity, and claimed to be an atheist.

When I first started showing the Colonel and his wife homes, he wrote to a banker friend of his back in a town where I taught and coached for my first four years, some thirty-odd years before. "I am now doing some real estate business with a man in Coldwater you undoubtedly knew some time ago, because he previously taught and was a coach in your community. His name is Floyd Eby, and I have checked him out down here. He seems to be all right, with only one weakness, he is real religious. Please write back and tell me what he was like when you knew him, because I don't want to be taken in on a real estate deal."

The banker friend wrote back, and said Eby was all right when he lived there.

It is amazing that an atheist who doesn't believe in a God of right and wrong, with guidelines to live an honest, happy, fruitful life, would fear being taken by another person.

I would never argue with the Colonel, but he kept poking remarks at me about my stupidity for believing in God and the Bible.

"Eby, I can't understand a man like you," he would remark. "A man who is intelligent enough to graduate from the University as a scientist, teacher, and coach; be a successful businessman, have a good professional position, and yet still be stupid enough to believe that nonsense called the Bible, God and Jesus. How can you think that way anyhow, and still hold onto your sanity?"

"I know it is true, Colonel," I said, "because God and the Bible changed my life completely, and I know it is true because I was there when it happened. This new way of life has also changed the lives of thousands of my friends."

The Colonel countered, "It is all in your mind. You believe what you want to believe. It really is a myth."

"I don't care what you call it, Colonel," I exclaimed, "But it has done the job for me and millions of others, and I know it is for real, and I have never been happier."

The Colonel kept after me every time I showed him houses. One day he said, "I stopped in the real estate office when you weren't there, and I started talking to the realtor's wife, Mrs. L. And you know, Floyd, she is worse than even you. You know what she told me?"

"What did she tell you, Colonel?" I asked.

"She told me that some day the Lord was coming down out of the sky, blow a trumpet, and whisk her up in the sky, and she would then be forever with the Lord," he exclaimed. "Did you ever hear of anything so queer?"

"Yes, Colonel, that is just the way I believe," I remarked.

"No, no, no," grunted the Colonel.

"Yes, yes, yes," I replied.

The Colonel never changed his mind, but he never failed to bring the subject up every time we met.

I was talking one day with one of our local coaches and teacher, and one of my former athletes, in a downtown parking lot. The Colonel came along, and I introduced him to Ben who is an outstanding Christian man.

The Colonel remarked, "I hope you haven't polluted this young man with your silly ideas about the Bible."

Immediately, Ben took him to task about the Bible and his own beliefs. A few minutes later, the Colonel stated, "This young fellow is nuttier than even you, Eby."

After showing the Colonel many houses over a sixty day period, I received a phone call early one morning. "Eby this is the Colonel from Battle Creek. My wife and I are coming down today at 11:00 a.m. to purchase that last house you showed us. That is the one we definitely want."

I had already committed my day to fly some needed Bibles up north. "Colonel, could you come tomorrow instead? I am going to be tied up today."

"What are you doing today, Eby?" he wanted to know.

"I am flying a large load of Bibles up north," I answered.

"We are going to be there today at 11:00 a.m. to buy that house -- and you will be there or you are going to lose your six hundred dollar commission," the Colonel raged. "If you are not, I am going to sign it up with one of the other salesmen, and even if they haven't done the work, they will receive the commission. Are you going to be there, or not?"

The Colonel was right. I would lose the commission. I was tempted, thinking that perhaps I could postpone my northern trip for a day by making some phone calls. However, God gave me the strength to tell the Colonel, "That is all right with me, but I must stick to my commitment to my Lord."

"That is stupid," replied the Colonel, and he hung up.

Although I fulfilled my commitment to God that day by flying the Bibles up north, most of the joy of serving Him was lost in the continual thought of the six hundred dollars I had lost, and in being envious of the salesman who was collecting it without working for it.

The next morning I received a phone call from Battle Creek. "Eby, this is the Colonel. Did you get through with your trip to the Gentiles? If you have, we are coming down to buy that house today."

"Didn't you buy it yesterday, Colonel?" I asked.

"No, but I am coming down today at 11:00 a.m. to buy it."

Just then, God revealed the truth to me. The Colonel had set a trap for me, and I almost walked into it. If I had postponed the Lord's trip to sell the house and collected the six hundred dollars, the Colonel would never have let me forget about it. In fact, he would have ruined my testimony by preaching all over the city that Eby pretends to be a Christian, but stick $600 in front of him and he, too, will deny his Christ.

I really shudder when I think of how close I came to falling into this trap, and becoming a stumbling block to others. Praise God that He led me away from the trap, and also took care of my financial needs.

Just recently I met the Colonel in the bank parking lot. As usual, I asked him how things were, and how he was getting along. He answered, "I used you as an illustration the other day, Floyd. One of my acquaintances performed a real foolish act yesterday, and I told him that was real stupid, but don't worry friend, I know another man in this community, Floyd Eby, who would make you look real intelligent. This Eby is so dumb that he believes in the Bible and God."

I just laughed.

Then the Colonel started telling me about all his problems. "Floyd," he said, "I just don't know what to do. My wife is real sick in a convalescent home. The doctors say there is absolutely no hope for her, and most of the time she doesn't even know me. I visit her, and it makes me sick to see her like that. Then I go home to that house you sold me, and without her there, I am lonely and sick. I really don't know what to do or which way to turn. I have seriously considered taking my own life and ending it all, but I feel that she still needs me around. Life is no longer worth living."

The more the Colonel spoke, the closer he came to tears. I felt sorry for him, but all I could do was pray for him. To this day he will not turn his life over to the only One who can eliminate his problems; his loneliness: Jesus! What a sad and accurate picture of a life without Jesus. A once proud Colonel and outstanding Marine with much responsibility and importance, a beautiful family, financial solvency, and everything he needed for a wonderful, happy, fruitful life -- except Jesus. The Colonel is the picture of everyone at some stage of their lives if they don't have Jesus. They, like the Colonel, are depressed, dejected, lonely confused, sick, doubting, with no security. Praise God, I have Jesus!

I Have Lost Everything

Jerry was an avowed atheist. He was married, with three fine daughters, all of them pre-school age. The family lived in a large, deluxe mobile home. One night, I talked to his wife at a home Bible study. She accepted the Lord, and joined the Family of God. Jerry resented this so-called "Jesus Freak" movement his wife was hooked on. Clara found it difficult to grow spiritually, and get close to God. Jerry resented her new way of life, so Clara gave up her Bible studies, Bible reading, prayer, and service of sending her girls to Sunday School.

I would stop in once in a while, and see how they were, and ask Clara if she was reading the Bible and praying. If Jerry was present, I would just chat with him a few minutes and try to make friends with him.

They moved their mobile home from the park, and I lost track of them, although I kept praying for the family, including Jerry.

A few weeks ago, early one Sunday morning, my door bell rang.

At the time, I was getting ready to fly out of town to speak at a church. I answered the door. Standing there was a forlorn, dejected, miserable Jerry -- after a bad night. I had known he was an alcoholic as well as a dope user. I told him to come in, and he came as far as my foyer. He said, "Coach, I have lost everything; my children and wife have left me, I have lost my job, my mobile home, my self-respect, and I no longer have any desire to live. I don't know why I came here."

"I know why you came here, Jerry," I said. "You see, I have been praying for over a year now that God, if it is within His Will, would send you here to talk with me."

Jerry and I went downstairs to my recreation room, and I opened God's Precious Word. I told him about God's Wonderful Plan for his life, and told him how simple it was to accept Christ as Saviour, and join the Family of God.

Jerry professed Jesus that Sunday morning and joined the Family. After taking his hand, we bowed our heads, and asked God's blessing on this new child of God, and his family. After closing in prayer, I asked Jerry to wait for me as I went upstairs to call Clara, his wife, who had moved to another city with her parents. Jerry told me it wouldn't do any good, because Clara wouldn't even talk to me about him. I told him that we would leave that up to God.

I reached Clara on the telephone that Sunday morning.

"Clara, this is Coach Eby. I just wanted to tell you that Jerry showed up here an hour ago, and has just now accepted Christ as Saviour, and joined the Family of God. I only ask one thing of you, Clara. Will you please pray for Jerry?"

She assured me that she would.

When I went back downstairs to Jerry I found him on his knees praying out loud to God with tears streaming down his cheeks.

Jerry started reading the Bible, attending Bible studies, praying, and meeting with other Christians.

About two weeks later, I met Jerry in the post office, and greeted him. He kind of hung his head, as he told me that he had gone off the "wagon."

I think he half expected to hear a lecture. I just said, "So what. God is able and He is forgiving. Just truly repent, and ask God's forgiveness and start over. As you continue to get closer to God, Jerry, by daily Bible reading and daily prayer, being with other Christians, and serving Jesus, He will eventually take it away from you."

Friends, Jerry needs to do the same thing that we all need to do, and this is to discipline ourselves to grow spiritually by disciplined Bible reading, disciplined prayer time, disciplined fellowship with other believers, and disciplined service to our Jesus.

Then God will step in and bless our lives by removing our problems.

Just try it if you don't believe it!

Wasting Your Time

I was working in my office one afternoon when I noticed a car pulling into my driveway. It backed out, and drove away. I thought someone was using my driveway to turn around. My phone soon rang, and the man at the other end of the line asked me if this was Coach Eby. I assured him that it was. The voice said, "Coach Eby, this is Gene, one of your former high school students many years ago. I am an alcoholic, and this problem is ruining my life and my family's life. I heard that you work with people with problems like this. I just drove into your driveway, but 'chickened out' and drove away."

I told him to come over if he desired, and we could talk as God opened the door.

A few minutes later, Gene was with me in my basement recreation room. I started talking to him about Jesus, but he interrupted me.

"Coach, I know all about that stuff. But that isn't what I need now. I need help with this alcohol problem. What about it?"

I asked Gene if he believed that God wrote the Bible in the original writings as He claimed He did.

"No," he answered, "I believe the Bible was written by men, and God didn't have anything to do with it."

I said, "O.K., let's forget about it. There is no use talking about spiritual help if that is what you really believe."

"Now, Coach, what about helping me with my alcoholic problem?" he asked. "You know I have been praying about this for hours and hours, praying that God would take away this problem that is ruining my life. Why doesn't He do it?"

"You are wasting your time, Gene," I said. "You can pray

to God until you're blue in the face, and you still will not get any help from God."

"Why not?" He wanted to know.

"Because God doesn't even hear you. On your own profession, you are not a child of God, because no one can be a child of God if they don't believe the Bible is God's Word, and written by Him in the original writings. So, don't waste your time praying, Gene."

Gene left and has never been back. I know he will never solve his problem until he turns his life over to the Living God!

The Mind Is God

Dan was one of the pillars of his church. He taught Sunday School class and directed the choir; was married with two children. One day he ran away with one of the girls in the choir, leaving his family, his church, and leaving his Christianity right in that church.

I was asked by some Christian friends if I would talk to Dan about his spiritual life. I said if they would pray about it, I would make contact, and see if God would open the door. I had never met Dan, and knew very little about him. I telephoned several times at his place of business, but never found him in. I reasoned that the Lord did not want me to talk with Dan, but I decided I would try to make one more attempt by letter.

I wrote to Dan describing something about myself. I told him if it would be all right, I would like to visit him about his "hang-ups" on Christianity. I was sure his "hang-ups" were the same as mine used to be. I enclosed a self-addressed, stamped envelope with my letter. After several weeks of not receiving an answer, and giving up on hearing from him, I received a letter. He stated that he didn't have any "hang-ups" on Christianity; he just didn't believe like I did. However, he said that I sounded interesting, and he would welcome a visit with me.

I flew to his city and met him at the airport restaurant, where we ate lunch together. After talking about business and other generalities, making friends with him and finding our mutual interests, I started talking to him about my faith in God. Dan began to tell me about his background and what he had done. I told him I wasn't interested in his past, but just in his future. However, he was not interested in professing Jesus and joining the Family of God.

I looked at him and asked, "Do you believe there is a God, Dan?"

"Not really, he answered. "I believe my mind is God, and that the mind can solve all things."

"Then there is no purpose, Dan, for us to talk about God and the Bible," I countered. "I will pray that my God will reveal himself to you as He has to me, and if that day ever comes, then we can talk about spiritual help and happiness."

"I hope you will come and visit again, Floyd, he said. "I want you to meet my new wife -- we will be marrying shortly. She will really give you a bad time about this religious bit."

As I left Dan on friendly terms, we agreed that we would visit again. So far, God has not opened the door, but I have faith that He will -- at the accepted time, and that Dan and his wife will enter the Kingdom of God! I praise God that I do not believe in atheism, a hopeless condition, but rather in a Living God who has all the answers to a happy, fruitful life.

> *"For the wisdom of this world is foolishness
> with God. For it is written, He taketh the
> wise in their own craftiness."*
> *I Corinthians 3:19*

> *"He stretcheth out the north over the empty
> place, and hangeth the earth upon nothing."*
> *Job 26:7*

SCIENTISTS DISCOVERING GOD

As a child, every night before I climbed into bed I would get on my knees and pray that God would make my mother well. My mother was a fine Christian lady, who played the piano at church, taught Sunday School class, and showed the love of Christ in her everyday life. However, mother was continually sick for ten years, in intense pain, many times even delirious. At that time, the doctors didn't have the necessary drugs to relieve the pain. My mother had four major operations and many other minor operations, but medical science could not diagnose her trouble.

After years of daily praying that God would make my mother well, she died. I was a freshman in college. God never made her well, and I hated God for that -- and for not answering my prayers. Just before mother died, she called me to her side, and asked me to promise that I would read the Bible, and because of my intense love for her, I gave her that promise.

But because of my hatred toward God for not making my mother well, I refused to read the Bible while I was in college, and this same hatred was instrumental in blocking my salvation. When I was praying about my mother, I didn't realize that I was not a child of God, and God didn't even hear my request. I finally learned that, to have my prayers answered, I first had to accept God as My Heavenly Father, and then pray to Him, not to some unknown creator that I didn't even know. Secondly, my prayers for my mother were somewhat selfish, as that was the only petition I ever prayed for, and I demanded of God -- not according to His Will.

Because of this hatred, and failure to read the Bible, I became a cynic, and more interested in science. I graduated from the university with a major in science with excellent grades in this field. I then believed that God and the Bible had to definitely take second place to science, and that science could be proven, but the Bible couldn't. Science, not the Bible, had all the answers.

After graduation, I taught science and coached in public high schools for five years. I then enlisted in the U.S. Navy during World War II, and after training, shipped overseas to a destroyer escort as a Communications Officer. While overseas, I became more confused about my relationship with God. I sometimes even thought I was a Christian, because of the decent life I had always lived and my early Christian training. However, I knew that something was missing, and I knew I was trying to ride the fence without falling off into atheism or Christianity.

Being by nature a decisive person, I detested this indecision about my relationship to God. I decided then and there that I was going to become an avowed atheist or a believer. I came to the conclusion that being a scientist, the most logical choice was to become an atheist. So I started to read the Bible in order to prove it wrong and become a good atheist.

Praise God, I got hooked on the Bible! I found that my righteousness was like filthy rags, and that good works would never get me into the Kingdom of God. In going through the scriptures, I soon had a personal encounter with Jesus, and He replaced science as my top priority, and since then God has been first, and science has been second. This is the only way that it can be if we are to be children of God, serve Him, and be abundantly blessed by our Saviour.

Redeeming The Time

Some of the top scientists in the United States are personal friends of mine. One of them is Dr. Harold Manner. The following is his personal testimony, published here with his permission because of his love for our Lord, Jesus Christ.

* * * * *

"I am Dr. Harold Manner and I am a scientist. More specifically I am a biologist, and for the past three years I have been chairman of the Biology Department at Loyola University of Chicago.

I would like to tell you a story that is extremely important. It is important to me because it happened to me. You know one of the most quoted verses in the Bible is John 3:16 -- 'For God so loved the world, that He gave His only begotten Son, that whosoever believeth in Him should not perish, but have everlasting life.' But as much quoted as that verse is, there is another part of the same book of John, the same chapter that means a lot to me, and I would like to use that as my text. If you will turn in your Bibles to John 3:1 - 7. *There was a man of the Pharisees, named Nicodemus, a ruler of the Jews. The same came to Jesus by night, and said unto Him, Rabbi, we know that thou art a teacher come from God; for no man can do these miracles that thou doest, except God be with him. Jesus answered and said unto him. Verily, verily, I say unto thee, except a man be born again, he cannot see the Kingdom of God. Nicodemus saith unto Him. How can a man be born when he is old? Can he enter the second time into his mother's womb, and be born? Jesus answered, verily, verily, I say unto thee, except a man be born of water and of the Spirit, he cannot enter into the Kingdom of God. That which is born of the flesh is flesh; and that which is born of the Spirit is spirit. Marvel not that I said unto thee, Ye must be born again.''*

"You know that was just a story to me until an extremely important meeting took place, a meeting between a loving Father and me and a Gideon placed Bible, and that is the story I would like to tell you this evening. In order to tell you the story properly, I must take you back to the early years of my life.''

I came from a small town in New Jersey. My parents were God-fearing parents, and Sunday around our house was truly the Lord's Day. To give you an example of how we would spend our Sunday, we would get up early in the morning and head off for church, and church was about ten miles away. We got there early because we went to Sunday School. My father and mother taught in the Sunday School and my sister and I attended. And after Sunday School, we all went to church where we sang in the choir.

Because so many of the parishioners lived quite a distance from the church, the choir director held the choir rehearsal immediately after church. And so sometimes it wasn't until one-thirty or two o'clock when we would finally get home for our Sunday dinner. After eating dinner, we had a short time for fellowship, and then back into the car and back to church. Because this happened to be a Presbyterian Church, and we had a young people's group called Christian Endeavour, my sister and I were both active in that. After the young people's meeting, we went to evening church and then finally home just about in time for bed. I want you to know that this wasn't just on Easter Sunday, or Christmas, or some other special religious day; that was each and every Sunday that I can remember.

In fact at this church they had an award system in Sunday School. The first year you got a pin and the second year of perfect attendance, you got a wreath to go around that pin, and each year of perfect attendance after that, you got a bar to hang onto these pins. Why, I tell you, by the time I was sixteen years old, I looked like a general walking into Sunday School in the morning.

So, it wasn't just a very unique Sunday, it was every Sunday. If anyone had said at the time, Harold, are you a Christian? I would have looked at him and thought that he was really out of his mind. Was I a Christian? Why, of course I was a Christian. Didn't I get up early in the morning? Didn't I go to Sunday School, and didn't I go to church, and didn't I sing in the choir, and didn't I take part in the young people's group, and didn't I go to evening church, and didn't I give up every single Sunday in my life? Sure, I was a Christian. But you know if I had answered that way, I would have been wrong. I know that today, because at the tender age of seventeen, we were beginning World War II

I joined the United States Navy, and the reason that I knew I wasn't a Christian was that whatever I was calling Christianity, I left right behind me in that church in that little town in New Jersey.

What I was doing for that sixteen or seventeen years is what so many people are doing in their churches today, and that is playing church. I certainly wasn't a Christian. When I went to boot camp, which was in Great Lakes, Illinois, I heard my first command that I wasn't familiar with, and that command was, *the smoking lamp is now lit.* Now for those of you who were in the Navy, you understand what that meant. There were certain areas that were prohibited in terms of smoking. There were certain times when smoking wasn't allowed. So when you were in a proper area and the time was right, they said the smoking lamp was lit. This meant everybody took out their packs of cigarettes and smoked. I wasn't a smoker, but I didn't have anything else to do, and it was boring, so I started to smoke. After I coughed through my first couple of cigarettes, I found I enjoyed it.

After boot camp, it was liberty, and there isn't a better town than Chicago for liberty. We headed out that gate and as sailors do, they usually head for the nearest bar. I went right along with them, and I took my first drink of whiskey. And I choked. It was the most horrendous taste that I had ever experienced in my life. But in spite of that, I learned to enjoy my whiskey. And it was a short step from there to women.

wine, women, and song; a girl in every port -- this was the motto of every sailor, and I did my part to hold up my end of that motto. In spite of all I was doing to myself at that time, I know today that looking down from Heaven was a loving Father who never stopped loving me, and who must have been saying, 'Harold, I still love you.' About halfway through my career in the Navy, I met a little girl. I don't know how her parents even allowed me to see her. There were times I would come to her house at night in a pitiful condition. I am sure I would not allow my daughters to see a man come into the house in that condition. Yet, they did, and again I knew it was God's doing because I grew to love that little girl, and I married her, and she is still my wife after thirty years. She has given me two wonderful daughters, and in turn they have given me grandchildren.

Soon the war was over and I was discharged. I went to college, and I was a little older, and a little more worldly than the majority of students in school, so I sat back and watched.

I heard the college professors who were teaching the biology courses telling the young people that they would have to make a choice. If they were going to be biologists, they had better give up all those fairy tales they had been reading in the Bible. They told the students science and religion just don't mix.

Let me digress just a moment, and let me say to you without condemning the whole profession that there is nothing more dangerous in our country today than a glib-talking professor in college. They can take a young mind, a beautiful mind, and they can twist it, and they can tear it, and they can distort it, and they can destroy that mind.

At any time I see a riot or an uprising of some kind at a college campus, I usually look deep and invariably I will find behind those young people, one or more of these college professors. And so I sat back and watched these young minds being destroyed.

This didn't bother me, because I had left any semblance of Christianity I might have had back in that church in New Jersey a long time ago.

After undergraduate school, I went to graduate school

where I earned my masters and my PhD degrees. In this school I watched the masterful teachers destroy whatever was left in the minds of these young people. Oh, they turned out to be fine biologists, there is no question about that. But they had a distorted view of everything else that was beautiful, or at least that was beautiful in their minds.

Then it was graduation day, and I was turned out. Now, I want you to notice something very carefully here. Up to this particular point in this story, everything that I had been doing had been affecting my salvation, my eternity, my mind, and my morality. But now at graduation, a real change came about because you see, now I became the college professor, and I am not proud of what I am going to say to you now, but I must say it.

During the first fifteen or sixteen years of my college teaching, I turned literally thousands of young people away from Jesus Christ; away from their love of God, away from all of those things that were serene and beautiful, that were taught to them by their parents.

I did this because I felt that I had to do it in order to turn out a good biologist. If you want to study with me, I would say, you had better leave that Sunday School material behind. I followed the same line my teachers fed me. If you want to be a scientist, you had better realize that science and religion just don't mix.

Then something happened.

Every year I go to a number of scientific meetings, and at these meetings, I usually go to the scientific sessions in the afternoon, come back to the hotel, get washed up, and dressed up, and go out on the town in the evening. I fully intended doing that at this particular scientific meeting at Washington, D.C. I went to the sessions in the afternoon and came back to the hotel.

But something was different because when I walked into the room, I saw lying open on the bed, a Gideon placed Bible. Now I can assure you that I had never opened a Bible in a hotel room. I had never opened a Bible in my life. I know, as a scientist, that there was an immediate explanation for that

Bible being opened. Some chamber maid undoubtedly needed spiritual help, so during the course of her duty, she opened the Bible to read a few passages, and in her haste to get to the next room she undoubtedly left it open.

But I know now that there was a prime mover and that prime mover was a loving Father who looked down on me and said, 'Harold, I still love you!'..In spite of what I had done, in spite of how many children I had turned away, there was still that Father who sang, 'I still love you.' I sat down and looked at that Bible, and I picked it up and it happened to be open to the Gospel of Matthew, the Sermon on the Mount, and I started to read, and I was fascinated.

Something struck me immediately. I realized in spite of all of those years of perfect attendance in Sunday School and church, I had never read the Bible. In Sunday School I would get a small four-page pamphlet with a colorful picture on the front and a Bible story on the inside.

In church, the Pastor would read two or three verses from the Bible, and then expound on it for the next twenty or twenty-five minutes, but never was I encouraged to read for myself the Word of God.

But in that motel room I read, and the more I read, the more fascinated I became. I can tell you by the time those meetings were over in Washington, I had read through the four Gospels. I was thrilled.

When I came home to St. Louis, my wife met me at the door, and after greeting me, asked how the meetings were. 'Fine, Doll,' I said, 'but get your coat.' 'Where are we going?' she asked. 'To the store,' I replied, 'to get a Bible.'

Now she thought I had really tied one on in Washington. But we went to the store, and we bought a Bible. Two dollars in change, I remember to this day. A red covered Bible, and one called a red letter edition, where everyting that Jesus said was written in red. I still have that Bible, and have many more in my home today, but that Bible has a very special place because it was the first Bible. What makes this even more rewarding for me is to realize that I had two teenage daughters at the time, and never in our house did we have a copy of the

Word of God, and these children were raised without the benefit of knowing the Word of God.

My life changed after that. I began listening to Christian radio stations; I began to read the Word of God more; I went to church, and came under the hand of a very wonderful pastor in St. Louis. A pastor who really believed that it was his job to feed his flock, and I was one of his flock. He taught me how to pray. He taught me how to listen for God's answers to my prayers. He told me about salvation and about being born again.

One evening at an altar call, I came forward, and something happened that had never happened before. While I was accepting Christ, tears began to roll down my cheeks. I am not normally an emotional person, but that day was one of the most fantastic days in my life. As those tears rolled down, I knew exactly how Paul must have felt on the road to Damascus. It was as if God were looking down and saying, 'Harold, now is the time.*Haven't you done enough to my young people? Isn't it time now you turned around, and brought some of those young people back to me?*' And I said, 'Yes, Father,' and at that point I dedicated my life to bringing people back to Jesus Christ, and through Jesus Christ bringing them back to God. It's been a very rewarding thing for me, and it's certainly been a change throughout my entire life. I want to thank a lot of people. I want to thank first of all, that pastor in St. Louis. Secondly, I want to thank the Gideons, because had it not been for the dedication of these men, that Bible would not have been in that hotel room, and I would not have been exposed to the very powerful, the very beautiful Word of God. But, above all, I want to thank a Father in Heaven, whose love was so great, whose love never stopped, whose love kept on in spite of what I was doing, because He knew that someday I would come back to Him. Thank you, Father! Thank you!

But you know it isn't all just a matter of thanks, because I still have burdens and joys. One of the burdens that I have is the fact there is so much trash in the form of textbooks going into our schools today. Let me quote from a textbook that is in a number of our colleges around the country. It is entitled General Biology, and it actually makes a mockery of God. It reads, 'Two main types of theories have been advanced to account for the origin of species. Either each species was created individually by some unseen, and presumably supernatural power or science is correct.' That bothers me as an individual, but it bothers me even more because I am the author of that textbook. So, as I go around the country winning more and more people to Jesus, my written word is still turning them away. So, I ask for your prayers that a book such as this will soon decrease in numbers around our college campuses.

But there is a joy that's come to my life as a result of all these things I have talked about. That is since my own conversion, my wife and two daughters have received Jesus as their personal Saviour."

* * * * *

Dr. John Moore from Michigan State University, a personal friend of mine, is a top scientist in the midwest. As previously mentioned, Dr. Moore was an avowed atheist until 1962, when he joined the Family of God by accepting Jesus as his Saviour. Dr. Moore has indicated through books and many lectures that he now believes, and accepts the Bible as God's Holy Inspired Word, and that it is accurate and reliable. According to Dr. Moore, the only time that the Bible and science disagree is when science is wrong. Many other scientists are now turning to God and His Word, the Bible for the ultimate truth.

My Science Teacher Says There Is No God

I flew to Midland, Michigan with a plane load of Bibles, and I wanted to store them in the terminal building until they could be picked up by different individuals to distribute throughout the state. The convention was the next day, and certain Gideons would pick them up at that time. I got out of my plane and walked into the building and asked the man in charge if I could store the Bibles in the building. Joe assured me that I could, and offered to help me carry the Bibles in from the plane. As we were carrying the Bibles in, I started talking to Joe about my faith in God.

"I am not a particularly religious man," he said, "but I would like to ask you some questions."

So we went into the office, and started discussing God's Word, the Bible.

"I am sort of up-tight about something that happened just recently," Joe said. "About a month ago, my ninth grade daughter came home from school and informed me that there wasn't such a thing as God. She said that her science teacher told her that no way could there be a God, and he could prove this as a fact. She told me she believed her science teacher and now knew that there was no God. Two weeks later, my seventh grade daughter came home from school and notified the family that she also no longer believed in God, as her science teacher also denied the existence of God. Even though I am not what you would call religious, these two incidents have irked me."

"Where do you live, Joe?" I asked. "About ten miles from here," he replied.

I asked him what time he would be home, and he told me 9:00 p.m.

"Joe, I am also a science teacher. What about me coming to your house and talking with your daughters after you arrive home?"

"I don't know about that," he answered. "I won't preach to them, Joe, and I will get along with them O.K."

"I have worked with young people almost all of my life," I countered.

He reluctantly agreed to let me come. I borrowed a car from a friend, and drove out to Joe's home at 9:00 p.m. Carrying an arm full of Bibles, I walked to the door and rang the bell. Joe wasn't home yet, and his wife answered the door. I didn't know her, and she didn't know me, and she wondered what I wanted. I introduced myself, and started trying to explain when Joe arrived.

Praise God! Joe invited me in and introduced me not only to his two daughters, but also to his two sons. I gave each one two Bibles each, and put their names in them. Then I started talking to them about how I found Jesus Christ even though I am a scientist. I let the girls know that their science teachers were wrong, and that not only I knew they were wrong, but many of my personal scientific friends would also declare them wrong. Then I explained to all of them why I knew the Bible was true and accurate, and also how it had changed my life. After going through the scriptures, each one professed Christ and joined the Family of God.

But I Don't Believe The Bible

I received a letter from a sociology class in Bronson High School inviting me to their class on a certain day to speak on morals, and answer questions. The letter promised that there would be much opposition. At first, I decided not to accept the invitation. Then I thought it might be God opening the door for some reason, so I wrote back and told them I would be there.

On that day, I spoke seventeen minutes on morals as related from the Bible, and then I allowed seventeen minutes for questions. Do you believe in wife swapping? Do you believe in pre-marital sex? Do you believe in abortion? Do you believe in homosexual relations? In communal living? These were some of the many questions fired at me. I said, "It doesn't matter what I believe. My opinions are worthless. But let us go to God's Word and find out what He says."

I read from Hebrews 13:4 *Marriage is honourable in all, and the bed undefiled; but whoremongers and adulterers God will judge.* I tried to answer each question from God's Word. The teacher sat back in the corner. I found out later that he claimed to be an atheist.

He spoke up, "Sir, you are always saying the Bible says this and the Bible says that, but that is no answer to me because I don't believe in the Bible."

"Sir," I said, "it doesn't make one particle of difference

that you don't believe in the Bible, because it is still true no matter what you believe. God doesn't change His Word just because of what you believe or do not believe. The Bible is always true no matter what *anyone* believes."

2 Timothy 3:16 *All scripture is given by inspiration of God, and is profitable for doctrine, for reproof, for correction, for instruction in righteousness.*

*So when they continued asking him, he
lifted up himself, and said unto them.
He that is without sin among you, let
him first cast a stone at her.*
John 8:7

7

RIGHT ON MAN

God Is Always Available

One morning at 3:30, my door bell rang. I struggled out of bed, and down the hallway, trying to gather my thoughts, and wondering who would be at my front door this time of the morning. Opening the door, I saw a young bearded man who asked, "Coach, do you remember me? I am Jeff."

"Yes, I remember the name," I replied. Jeff had been one of my high school students several years ago.

"Coach, you told us in high school that we could call on you at any time if we ever had problems, and I have problems," he said.

"Sure, Jeff, come on in," I countered.

"I have four more out in the car that also have problems," Jeff continued.

"Well, bring them all in," I invited.

Four young men and one young lady walked into my living room and sat down, and started telling me about their problems: living in a commune, dope, alcohol, and many others.

"Just a minute," I said. I went into my office and picked up five testaments, and gave one to each and told them, "I can't help you with your problems, but I can introduce you to Jesus. He can give you a Way of Life that will eliminate all these problems. There is no charge and no obligation, and if you don't like what I say, just say, 'turn off, Coach,' and I will stop."

So that morning at 3:30 in my living room, I opened up God's Word. I told these five young people about God's Wonderful Plan for their lives, and how He could give them a happy, fruitful life, if they would only join the Family of God, and become a close friend of Jesus. At 5:30 those four young men and the young lady accepted Christ as Personal Saviour and joined the Family of God.

I call them my 3:30 group. You can guess why. This group was responsible for me starting Home Bible Studies weekly for people with problems, where they could come to a designated home at a certain time, and read and discuss the Word of God. Each Wednesday, in Coldwater, Michigan, I have five different studies at five different homes ranging from 7:00 p.m. to midnight.

One night as I flew home at midnight, my wife had left a message on my desk to call Jeff, no matter how late it was, so I gave him a ring. Jeff answered, "Coach, I wrecked my panel truck tonight, and I don't know what to do. I lost control and rolled over in a ditch, with at least seven hundred dollars of damage, and I have no insurance. Why should this happen to me, why would God allow this to happen...I just don't understand why God would do this to me. I asked Jeff if anyone got hurt, and he said, "No." So I told him to put it in the hands of the Lord and go to bed, and I hung up.

This panel truck without windows, except the windshield, was Jeff's pride and joy. The next day Jeff came over to see me. "Coach," he said, "I know why God allowed this to happen to me and my truck."

"Why, Jeff?" I inquired.

"Because," he answered, "most of my sins are wrapped up

in that truck. That is the place we have our dope parties, and our beer and wine parties. It is where we store our dope and alcohol, it is where I have a bed for the girls I take out, and I just know that God is telling me that He is displeased." Jeff went on to say that he had already removed the bed, the wine, and the dope.

One night I was visiting Jeff at his home, and before I left, Jeff said he had something for me. He went into his bedroom, and brought out a red hospital testament. He had stolen it from the hospital, and asked me if I would take it off his hands, because his conscience had been bothering him since he had been saved. I told him to keep reading it, I didn't want it. However, I was conducting a home Bible study one night and Jeff was present, along with a young lady from Kentucky. After she accepted Christ, I asked Jeff to ask God's blessing on this new sister in Christ, which he did. Then he also asked me to take that red hospital testament. I did, and still have it.

God's Mysterious Ways

Before flying to Detroit one night to speak at a meeting, I checked with the weatherman. He gave me clearance of VFR flying weather until midnight, after which it was supposed to rain intensely. Coming out of the meeting at 10:00 p.m., I found the bad weather had moved in early. It was raining hard. I called the weatherman, and he informed me that VFR flying was out of the question. I asked him about the next day, and he said it would be bad until 11:00 a.m., and then it would clear up so VFR flying would be permissible. I praised God for this report, because this would give me time to fly home the next day. I could then pick up my wife, and fly to Petoskey, Michigan by mid-afternoon, where I had Christian commitments at that time. I stayed over night in Detroit with a friend, and the next morning at 6:00 a.m., I called the weatherman and he informed me that there would be no VFR flying all day or night. The weather had settled in and was not moving out that day. I knew I was stuck and I was going to have to make other arrangements. Reluctantly, I called the bus station and checked the schedules. They had a bus that would arrive in Marshall, Michigan at 11:00 a.m. I called my wife and asked her to meet me with the car at Marshall at that time and we would drive from there to Petoskey.

As I boarded the bus in Detroit, I was grumbling to myself about this situation, and trying to throw the blame on my Lord. I asked the Lord why He allowed this bad weather situation to come up? Certainly, He wanted me in Petoskey to do His work. Certainly, He could have held off the bad weather until I could have flown home. This situation is ridiculous, Lord, I thought. I have to leave my plane in Detroit, take the bus to Marshall, and drive fast to Petoskey to meet my commitment to the Lord's work by mid-afternoon. Then, in a couple of days, after coming back from Petoskey, I would have to select a flying day, take the bus back to Detroit, and fly my plane home to Coldwater. How much inconvenience do you allow to happen, Lord, for me to serve You? I walked down the aisle of a crowded Greyhound bus still grumbling. Finding an empty seat next to a young lady, I asked her if I could sit down. She seemed to be half asleep, but she nodded her head. I sat down and she seemed to go back to sleep.

Lord, what is the purpose of having me on this silly bus? Is it to witness to this young lady? When she awoke I found that her name was Jean; that she was originally from Battle Creek where she went to high school; that after graduation she went to Detroit where she was now working. Jean was now traveling back to Battle Creek to go to her grandfather's funeral. I happened to know some of the coaches and teachers she had in high school and after some conversation, I seemed to have her confidence and friendship.

Eventually, Jean told me that she had been on dope in high school and afterwards. Her life had been a mess. Recently she had felt the need to clean up her life, but didn't quite know how to go about it. I pulled a personal worker's testament out of my pocket, wrote her name in it, and presented it to her as a gift, and she accepted it.

I told Jean how I had found a New Way of Life that is

tremendous. Though at one time I had not believed the Bible, I now believed it one hundred per cent. I explained to her the four reasons why I now believe the Bible, and she said those reasons also made sense to her. I then had her read the salvation verses out loud to me, and I explained them to her. After about forty minutes of reading, discussion, and prayer, Jean joined the Family of God, and accepted Jesus as her Saviour.

I told Jean that she could put the small testament in her purse, but she informed me that she wanted to read it. She continued to read verses out loud to me. Jean told me that her brother in high school was hooked on heroin, and her father was an alcoholic. She wanted to know how she could witness to them. After some discussion, we decided that she would buy and present to her father and brother, a Bible as a gift. She would pray for them, and she herself would try to get as close to God as she could. I left Jean at Marshall, where my wife picked me up with the car, and we proceeded to Petoskey.

Two weeks later, I received a letter from Jean from Detroit. She was depressed and everything was going wrong. She felt life was really not worth living, and she didn't know what to do.

I was scheduled to be in Pontiac at an early morning Gideon meeting the coming Saturday. At this meeting, I asked the Gideons to pray for Jean, that I might be able to locate her, and that God could use me to encourage her to get close to God.

After the meeting, I started out with my car to locate Jean, and after some searching I located the apartment where she supposedly lived with a girl friend.

I rang the door bell, and a girl by the name of Betty came to the door, informing me that she was Jean's roommate. She told me that Jean had worked until 2:00 a.m., and wasn't up yet. I told Betty to tell her that Coach Eby would be back to see her at 11:00 a.m. I went downtown and killed a couple of hours, then went back to the apartment, and once again Betty answered the door bell. Betty invited me in and led me upstairs to the apartment where I saw Jean and three boys.

I sensed that I had invaded a commune. Immediately I went over to the nearest boy and grabbed his hand and shook it and said, "My name is Coach Eby from Coldwater, Michigan. What is your name?"

He looked astounded, but answered, "Craig."

I then went to the other boys, and went through the same procedure. I exclaimed, "I am sorry fellows, but I didn't have time to get a haircut before I came."

This broke them up, as they realized the difference between their beards and long hair, and my establishment haircut and shaven face. I then greeted Jean and also shook Betty's hand.

I sat down and started some general conversation, asking about each one of them, and telling them about myself. I wasn't sure why Jean had five of them present when she knew I would be visiting her at 11:00 a.m. I thought perhaps she had a crowd to prevent me from talking to her about spiritual things. The other two boys' names were Bob and Bart. God then opened the door when one of the boys, Bart, asked me what I did for a living.

"I give away Bibles, free," I said. "The price is right. Isn't that great? Would you take one, Betty? She reluctantly said, "Yes."

"What about you, Bob and Craig?" I asked. They agreed, but without any sign of eagerness.

Bart decided that he wouldn't be the only non-conformist, and Jean had given the one I gave her on the bus to her brother in Battle Creek.

"I will be right back," I said. And I raced downstairs and out in the street to my car and picked up five testaments.

I went back upstairs, and wrote their names as I presented one to each. As I asked each one how to spell his or her last name, I heard Jean whisper to Bart, "You know why he wants your name? He is going to pray for you. That is what he did with me."

"That is right, Jean," I said. "And you are praying for me too, aren't you?"

She nodded yes.

"I am going to pray for Bart, but he can't pray for me unless he joins the Family of God like you did, Jean," I said. "It doesn't seem fair for me to pray for Bart, and he not for me. It looks like Bart ought to join the Family of God, so he can also pray for me."

Jean agreed, but Bart didn't say anything.

I now knew that Jean had the three boys and Betty present so I could tell them about Jesus.

Craig was crippled. He walked with crutches, and his body was deformed. I started the five of them reading the salvation verses, explaining to them God's love and compassion for each one of us.

Craig, the cripple, interrupted, "If this Almighty God you are telling us about is so full of love and compassion for me, why did He give me such a pitiful, crippled, deformed body like this?"

"I am glad you asked that question, Craig," I replied. "According to the Scriptures, God has promised you a new body within a short time, a perfect body like His own -- a body that is not crippled or deformed -- a body that will never deteriorate or have any pain or disease. All you have to do, Craig, to receive this promised new body, is to join the Family of God, by trusting and having faith in Jesus as your personal Saviour."

When we completed discussing the necessary steps to take, according to the Bible, to join the Family of God, Craig was the first of the four to accept Him. Then Bob and Betty also professed their faith in Jesus Christ. But Bart, who was Jean's boyfriend, would not take the step of faith. He wanted to question the Bible. I told Bart that he had a perfect right not to join the Family of God, and I would not "bug" him. God gives everyone a free choice, and no one has to go to Heaven if he doesn't want to.

I have continued to visit this commune. Two new members, Bruce and Doreen have also joined the Family of God. Jean and Bart moved out and got married and live in an apartment of their own.

One afternoon I visited the apartment and the only ones still there were Betty and Bob. I fell in love with all members of this commune, and they also accepted me. Several times they asked me to stay for a meal and even offered to put me up overnight. I always politely refused. Bob and Betty were partners. Betty told me if I didn't stay for supper, she would be mad at me, so I agreed.

I was pleasantly surprised when Betty prepared and served a fine meal.

I remarked to Bob, "It surprises me that you don't get fat, the way Betty feeds you."

"I only get this when Floyd Eby come," Bob replied.

As we were eating, Bob started pumping me about my opinions.

"Coach, you know that Betty and I are living together without being married," Bob poked at me.

"Is that so," I nonchalantly replied.

"You know it is so," Bob countered. "What do you think about it?"

"I don't think anything about it, Bob. It is none of my business. That is between you, Betty and the Lord."

"I want to know your real opinion on it," Bob insisted.

"I don't want to tell you my opinion, Bob, because as I said before it is none of my business, and it is none of your business what my opinion is."

Bob would not be denied. "You are my friend, and I insist on you giving me your opinion on this because I want to know."

"O.K., Bob, since you are insisting, I will give you my opinion. You know, I don't believe God is so concerned over a piece of paper called a marriage license. I am sure that occasions arise where couples do not have available a license and someone to marry them. I do believe that if a couple is living together under God, without the marriage ceremony, then our Lord would expect them to assume the same responsibility in their marriage without a ceremony as if they had a ceremony. That would include being faithful to our mate."

Immediately Betty spoke up, "I told you, Bob. That's your trouble. You want your cake and you want to eat it too."

That ended the discussion on that subject.

Bart would not join the family of God, and eventually Jean and Bart split. After the split, Bart made a profession to join the Family of God. He would not take the necessary steps to get close to God, so God could change his life, and the marriage ended in divorce. However, Jean is continuing to get closer to God and I am convinced that our Lord is going to give her a happy, fruitful life in Jesus.

It Is Possible

Dick and Ruth were involved in dope, alcohol, communal parties and living, and other anti-social activities. They became close friends, and Dick, through some records, a vision, and the reading of the Word, was saved. Not long after that, he was able to lead Ruth to Jesus.

Their lives started changing, and soon they were married. They purchased a mobile home of their own as Dick was now working regularly at a job.

On their honeymoon, they attended a church in Mackinaw City where I was speaking on a Gideon Assignment. After the message, I was greeting the people at the rear of the church, when Dick and Ruth came up and introduced themselves to me, and wanted to talk with me. They told me about their past lives, and how they had joined the Family of God. How thrilled they were to hear the testimonies of how God's Word was changing the lives of people.

The man counting the Gideon offering called me over.

"You know that young couple you were talking with came up and put $50.00 cash in the Gideon offering," he said. "I thought you would like to know that."

I praise a God that can transform lives like Dick and Ruth. A young couple living a "hippie type" life, who after Jesus came into their lives, were willing to shorten their honeymoon to purchase Bibles to tell others about their precious Jesus. Certainly the fifty dollars cash could have given them two extra days on their honeymoon.

Dick and Ruth and I became close friends after that and we

visited each other when we could. Whenever we met, we would spend time together in the Scriptures, prayer, and talking about Jesus. Both of them wanted me to come up and visit with their parents about Jesus.

They planned on a certain Sunday to invite the four parents over to their mobile home for dinner, and I was to be there. It was agreed they would tell their parents in advance that a friend of theirs wanted to also talk to them about the Bible and spiritual things.

But how to get the parents to attend on that basis was another problem.

The three of us decided to completely turn it over to the Lord, and to pray each day that the Lord would have the parents there if it was His will.

The day arrived, and all four parents were present. After a fine meal, prepared by Ruth and Dick, and after I had become acquainted with the four parents, I pointed out how proud they must be in the way Dick and Ruth's lives had been changed. All four agreed that the changes were all for the better. I told them how God and His Word, the Bible, had been responsible for changing not only Dick and Ruth's lives, but also my own. I opened the Bible, and explained how it had happened -- how this same God and Bible could change anyone's life -- if we took the necessary steps. All seven of us went through God's Plan for our lives as presented in the Scriptures. After that, we were all joined closely together as brothers and sisters in Christ, because we all belonged to the Family of God.

Dick and Ruth are joined with a church, sing in the choir, attend Bible study, read the Bible, pray, are with other Christians, and are serving Jesus. Just recently, God has blessed them with a beautiful son. Dick and Ruth also serve our Jesus by witnessing to many of their old friends, and many of their new friends. I praise God for my friends, Dick and Ruth, and their parents, and for the way that all of them have enriched my life.

Peter therefore was kept in prison;
but prayer was made without ceasing
of the church unto God for him.
Acts 12:5

8

GOD IS BEHIND BARS

God Forgives

Sometime ago, Zandy was thrown into the county jail for torturing to death her eighteen month old daughter.

A local Pastor called and told me that he believed that I was God's man to go up to the jail and talk to this young woman.

I really didn't want to go. It was repulsive to me to think that anyone would do such a thing. Then I thought of David in the old testament, and the Apostle Paul in the new testament, and Floyd Eby in modern times. What rascals they all were until they surrendered their lives to God.

Arriving at the jail, I received permission from the sheriff to take Zandy into a private room. I understood that Zandy could speak a little broken English and could understand a little English, but could only read Spanish, so I had brought along a Gideon placed Spanish new testament. I put Zandy's name in it, and my name, address, and telephone number, and gave it to her as a gift. She accepted it.

I didn't talk to Zandy about her problems, whether she was guilty or not, and how it happened. I only talked to her about Jesus, because only Jesus could help her with her problems, I couldn't. I asked Zandy to read Romans 3:23, Romans 6:23, John 1:12, and Revelation 3:20. Zandy read them in Spanish and I repeated the verses in English, and explained the meaning of the verses in simple English. About forty minutes later with tears of joy streaming down her cheeks, Zandy entered the Family of God by accepting Jesus as her Saviour, and we prayed together asking God's forgiveness and blessing on this new child of God.

I visited Zandy seven times after that at the jail, and each time as we read the scriptures, discussed the verses, and prayed, Zandy would cry with joy. She would say, "Brother Eby, I wish you would come more often. When you are not here, the prisoners make fun of me and I get so depressed and feel so bad. When you are here with me talking to me about Jesus, I feel the Holy Spirit, and feel so good, won't you come more often?"

After the seventh visit, I picked up my daily paper at home and read where Zandy had been deported to her native country of Panama.

Zandy had been deported, but she also had been promoted to a child of God through Jesus Christ our Lord.

Before Zandy left for Panama, she asked me to visit with her husband, Greg who was in the same jail on the same charge. I told her I would if he wanted to see me. I asked the turn key to ask Greg if he wanted to talk to Coach Eby about spiritual things.

I emphasized to the turn key that I didn't want to see Greg unless he wanted to see me. I did not know the man. The turn key came back and said, "Greg said there was no way that he wanted to talk with you. In fact he wanted absolutely nothing to do with you."

I thanked the turn key and told him that was fine.

Zandy kept "bugging" me to see Greg. She kept claiming that he wanted to see me. I explained to her that he refused to see me and that was his right of choice. After three weeks more of Zandy's persistence, I once again asked the turn key to ask Greg the same question. God had Greg prepared. Zandy was right. Greg was very anxious to talk with me, and he also joined the Family of God by accepting Jesus. His final question was, "What happened to my little daughter?"

I answered, "According to the scriptures, she is safe in the arms of our Jesus, and if you really put God first in your life, you will see her in Heaven."

On the very first day I visited Zandy, and she accepted Christ, I told her if she had a spiritual problem in the future, and all problems are spiritual to the Christian, that she could write to me or call me collect. I would then visit her as the Lord opens the door.

One night at 10:30 p.m. I received a person to person collect call from the country of Panama.

"Brother Eby this is Zandy," she said. "I just had to call you and let you know that I am praying for you and others each day like you said I should. I am telling my friends and relatives about Jesus like you said I should; I am reading that Bible every day like you said I should; and I have now joined a church and am serving Jesus every day like you said I should."

Yes, friends, it was worth the ten dollars and forty cents that the phone call cost, just to be once again assured that our Lord can change the worst of sinners if we just put our faith and trust in Him. I do not know if I will ever see Zandy again on this earth, but I feel certain I will see her in Heaven when that glorious day comes.

None of That Jesus Bit

One evening at 10:30 p.m., I received a phone call from one of my former students. He asked me if I knew that Carl and Merle were in jail. They were also two of my former students. I told him I hadn't heard, but I would try to visit them the next day.

Arriving at the jail the next day I asked the deputy if Carl and Merle were in jail.

He answered, "They sure are and that is where they belong and that is where they are going to stay."

I asked him if I could visit with them? "Are you a preacher?" he asked. I said no, and he notified me that I couldn't see them. I did think it was unusual that you had to be a preacher to get into jail. I told the deputy that I wanted to see the sheriff, and he let me know that the sheriff wouldn't be at the jail until 11:00 a.m. I told him I would be back at that time. After greeting the sheriff whom I knew, I asked him if I could visit Carl and Merle. The sheriff answered, "I can't break the rules, Coach, but I will make you a special consultant, and you can come and go as you want. You go into that room there, and I will bring them in." According to the sheriff, Carl and Merle had beaten up on a policeman and another adult.

When the sheriff brought Carl and Merle in the room, they obviously had also been beaten. Their eyes were swollen shut, both were limping badly, and the two were a motley looking couple with their long straggly hair and beards. Carl and Merle couldn't see me because their eyes were swollen shut.

One of them asked, "Who are you?"

"I am Coach Eby," I replied.

"Oh, Coach Eby," one of them exclaimed, "You came down to bail us out. It will take eight hundred dollars each, and we need to get out now so we can kill that policeman and that other adult."

"I didn't come down to bail you out," I replied. "I came to tell you about Jesus."

"One of them swore, and said, "We don't want any of that Jesus bit, we just want to get out so we can do what we have to do - kill those two guys."

"That will only get you into Jackson prison," I predicted.

"Just bail us out and let us kill those guys, and you can then come up to Jackson prison and talk to us about that Jesus bit," they said.

I told them that would be too late, and I took them both by the shoulders and pushed them down into chairs.

"You are going to hear about Jesus now whether you like it or not, and I am going to tell you what Jesus did for you and me," I said. "Now listen. You know they took Jesus and made Him carry a large wooden cross up the hill even though He collapsed and had to have help. Then they laid the cross on the ground, and laid Jesus on that cross, and pounded nails through His Hands and His Feet nailing Him to that cross. Picking up the cross, they chucked it into a hole and allowed Jesus to hang there by the nails in His hands and feet. They also stuck a spear in His side and allowed the blood to drain out of His Body, and He hung on this cross for hours until He died a tortured death."

Carl said, "That was worse than they treated us."

"It sure was," I answered, "And I don't know about you fellows, but I know that Jesus didn't deserve this torture. He did it for you and me so our sins could be forgiven, and we could have eternal life."

"We don't want to hear any more about it," they replied. "Just go bail us out."

I left Carl and Merle. I went home and into by bedroom, and on my knees I prayed that my God would not let them out of jail until He changed their hearts.

Unbeknown to me, a judge from Battle Creek came over and dismissed the bail and let them out. I had already called the adult and warned him of the hate in these two boys' hearts. However, God had touched their hearts---and when Carl and Merle were released, instead of hunting up the policeman and adult, they came to my home and we went down into the basement and talked about Jesus for over two hours. Even though both Carl and Merle need to get much closer to God, I am happy to report that both of them were enrolled in a Bible College.

Carl came to me one day and wanted to talk to me. "Coach, I am depressed, up tight, and confused," he said. "I just know that I am going to Hell and I just know I am not a Christian. No way can God forgive all the sins I have been committing. I just know that I am not a child of His, and I am headed straight to Hell, and I just feel terrible."

"Carl, I believe sincerely that you are a child of God," I quietly said. "If you were not a Christian, I don't believe all this sinning would bother you. You see, Carl, God is chastising you and making you feel terrible, because you are displeasing Him with your actions. You need to get closer to God, Carl, by reading the Bible more regularly, praying more often, being with other Christians regularly, and serving Jesus. Then He will lift the load off your shoulders."

Carl found out that this is true.

Appointment With Death

At a Gideon International Convention, I met and took out for dinner a black Gideon from a small overseas country with a population of several million inhabitants. This Gideon friend was in charge of all of the prisons in his country. He was not a Christian, but picked up one of the old Bibles in one of his prisons, and started to read it. After some time of reading, the Holy Spirit entered his life and he became a Christian by accepting Jesus as Saviour. My friend had a heavy burden for all the inmates of his prisons who were not believers, especially those on death's row awaiting execution by hanging.

The Gideon Jail Administrator would personally visit each and every inmate in every prison who was awaiting execution. He would take the Bible and tell them about God's Plan for their lives, and how they could have eternal life through Jesus Christ our Lord. Many accepted Christ and eternal life, but many rejected God's gift. Many of those who rejected Christ bragged that waiting for their execution didn't bother them at all. They would go to the gallows as they would go to the circus, and with a strong display of courage.

However, as my Gideon friend, the chief administrator of all prisons, would watch them go to the gallows, nearly every one of the unbelievers would break down in the last few minutes, become hysterical, and beg for their lives. The believers who had accepted Jesus as Saviour would walk up to the gallows praising God that they were thrown into jail where they had

had the opportunity of joining the Family of God, since the Gideon Administrator had opened the scriptures and told them about Jesus and Heaven. I praise God that I had a small part in sending the Bible overseas that brought this jail administrator to a saving knowledge of Jesus Christ and gave him the burden to tell others on death row about a wonderful loving God who will forgive if we truly repent; a God who even set us free from the gallows.

You Cannot Mock God

Kim joined the Family of God as I had the opportunity of talking with him while in jail. He received a two year sentence and was transferred to Michigan State Prison in Jackson. He had several children by his wife from whom he had been separated for some time, and several other children by his girl friends.

While in prison, Kim read the Bible, prayed, and sometimes had Bible studies with other inmates. Because of good behavior, he was transferred to Camp Shingleton in the upper pennisula where I flew to visit him. He had some problems with some of the inmates. They would ridicule him and wanted to fight him because Kim refused to enter into their underground activities of dope and alcohol.

Kim knew if he was caught in such activities, he would be sent back to the "big house" and receive an extension to his term. He became very depressed and lonely wanting to see his girl friend and some of his children. One night he ran away from camp with the intention of hitchhiking home to his girl friend and his children. As he was walking through the woods, God spoke to his heart and he pulled out his small testament. There was still enough light left that he read some verses of scripture. God led him back to the camp and he was still able to go back to quarters before he had been missed.

Because of his good behavior, he was transferred to Camp Waterloo, northeast of Jackson, where he had much freedom. I was able to visit with him and talk to him about the Bible and the Lord. Later on he was able to leave the camp each day with a work permit, and worked on an outside job where he made good money. He was allowed only a small amount for spending money, and the prison saved the rest in his account. Because of his continued good behavior, and a promise of a job that I had located for him, Kim was released on probation. He was given twelve hundred dollars that the prison had saved for him from his job.

I met with Kim as I took him to his job, and spent some time talking with him. I gave him an outline of a spiritual program to follow: Daily Bible Reading, daily prayer, be with other Christians, serve Jesus as He opens the door, contact all people to whom he owed honest debts and arrange to pay them back in small monthly amounts, weekly Bible study attendance, and weekly church attendance.

I told Kim if he followed this spiritual program, God would bless him and he would be assured of never going back to prison. I also told him that if he didn't follow this spiritual program, I could guarantee that he would go back to prison.

"Kim," I said, "I am not going to bug you about following this spiritual program or even check on you to see if you are following it. I am going to leave it entirely up to you. I will know if you follow it or not by whether you go back to jail or not."

Kim vowed that he was going to follow the program. But he didn't.

Kim had it too good. He had a job, only a 11:00 p.m. curfew, practically all of his freedom, and an ex-con woman. Instead of using the twelve hundred dollars to pay some of his honest debts and child support, he bought a car, which was against his probation regulations, quit his job, and took off from the state. Within a year, he was located and once again put into Jackson prison.

Kim and his new girl friend wanted me to visit him again, accept his collect phone calls again, and to help his girl friend locate transportation to visit him.

I wrote to Kim and through the love of Christ, I tried to communicate to him that God had given him a real opportunity and Kim had "blown" it.

God and I would still forgive him if he was truly sorry, but now the responsiblilty was on his own shoulders to prove to God that he was really sincere about his relationship with Jesus. I told Kim I would continue to write to him, pray for him, and when he was once again released, I would work with him again on a spiritual program. However, I told him at that time I needed to spend my time, effort and money on others who had not had the first chance.

I received a nasty letter back from Kim.

But I replied, telling him that I loved him and God loves him. I also reminded him that he could "con" me, but he couldn't "con" God, and I left him with Galatians 6:7 "Be not deceived; God is not mocked; for whatsoever a man soweth, that shall he also reap."

Many people inform me that the prisoners are just "conning" me when I talk to them about Jesus, just in order to get help. I always reply that is none of my business, because they cannot "con" God. I am doing what God would have me do, and the results are up to each individual and the Holy Spirit. God is blessing me as I am available to be used in any way He wants to use me. Praise God!

Prayed My Way Out

Casey has a wife and a two year old daughter. He had spent seven months in the county jail when I talked to him about Jesus, and he joined the Family of God. I saw Casey at jail services on Sundays, and visited with him privately several times. I also visited his wife and daughter occasionally. He started praying to God that he would be released so he could serve Him.

Even though it seemed certain that Casey was going to receive several years' sentence at Jackson, God saw fit to put him on probation.

I was present with Casey and Janet at the trial, so the court could use me as a secondary probation officer. After the court session, we sat in the office of the probation officer who went over all the rules with Casey, Janet and me. He told Casey, "If you don't like these rules, you don't have to obey them. We can send you to Jackson Prison instead. But if you want to stay out of prison, then you will obey them."

Casey and his family are now reading the Bible, attending church regularly, praying, and serving the Lord by driving the church bus for Sunday School, youth trips, and for daily vacation Bible school. Janet is helping Casey to organize the route, and call for new riders. Casey has a job, in spite of a handicap, and God is blessing their lives.

From Jail To Missionary

After being released from jail where he had received Christ as personal Saviour, Dave went home to Indiana. Joining the Family of God became a reality in Dave's life as he started attending some Christian activity each and every night. He also started witnessing to friends and acquaintances, as well as going to convalescent homes for visiting and witnessing. I am continually receiving letters from Dave, praising God for His love and compassion for himself and others. Dave is now a real missionary, witnessing, and working in a church camp.

Soon after his release, Dave wrote me a letter about his sister, Connie, who had many problems, including dope. Connie was nineteen years old, and Dave told me that she was headed down exactly the same road he had traveled. Connie would end up in jail also, if God didn't intervene. Dave sent me a picture of Connie and asked me to pray for her. I placed the picture on my prayer board, prayed for her, and also wrote her a letter. I told her who I was, and how I knew her brother, Dave. I told her that my wife and I had a way of life that was just tremendous, and that if she wanted me to, I would fly down and tell her about it. I had warned Dave not to "bug" Connie, but just pray for her, get as close to God as he possibly could so Connie would notice the real change in his life, and not to push her, or criticize her.

I was really surprised to receive a letter from Connie stating that she would like to see me and talk with me. I flew down to Kendallville airport, and Connie and her Aunt Eve met me there. I took both of them for an airplane ride, and even though it was Connie's first time in a plane, she was not scared, but enjoyed the flight.

When we landed and parked the plane, we stayed in the plane, and I gave both Connie and Eve two Bibles each. I started talking to them about this wonderful way of life my wife and I enjoyed. As I opened the scriptures, and had each one of them read, I discussed God's Wonderful Plan for their lives. Both Connie and Eve agreed to the necessary steps, and joined the Family of God. I was also invited to talk to a relative, a fifteen year old girl who had run away from home, and had many problems. June also accepted the Lord, and joined the Family of God.

Recently, I was flying to Indianapolis and I landed at the Auburn airport and met Connie there. We spent an hour going over the scriptures and talking about Jesus. It is thrilling to see how rapidly God is changing Connie's life. She is now attending church and singing in the choir, and going to Christian meetings during the week. Her old friends kept after her to come to their parties and she did for awhile, but when she continued to refuse to take dope, they quit inviting her, and now she prays for them. Connie now has several Christian friends she loves, who are helping her keep close to God. I praise God for this friend of mine and praise God for changing her life.

When Dave was first released from jail, his old buddies came around and coaxed him to party with them. When he would not do the things he used to do; the things his buddies still wanted him to do, they ridiculed him and made fun of him. This almost drove Dave back to his old ways. But one day when his buddies were picking on him, he stood up, and said, "Sure I am a Christian. Sure I am going to Heaven. Sure I love Jesus. Sure I am not going to displease Him, because He loves me and has given me a life worth living." After that his old buddies didn't want to have anything to do with him.

Why Don't You Shut Your Mouth?

The county jail had been having a lot of trouble with many inmates, mainly due to the crowded conditions. There was an overflow of inmates from outside the county. Because of these problems, we were not allowed to invite into one large cell all who desired to attend Sunday church service. Instead we had to go along the catwalk, and stop and talk to only those cell mates who wanted to hear us.

The first cell I approached had four young men in it. Two stood up to greet me, one other was seated on his bunk reading a comic book, and the other was sleeping on his lower bunk. I had to talk through the bars.

"I am here to talk to you about the Bible, Jesus, and a way of life; if you don't want to hear it, say so now, and I will go to the next cell," I said.

The two inmates who were standing near the bars indicated to me that they would like to listen, so I started talking to these two young men about the Bible. The young man on the lower bunk awakened, and hollered at me, "Why don't you shut your mouth?"

"I got the message, I will go to the next cell," I replied.

"Nothing doing," said one of the men with whom I had been talking. "He doesn't have to listen -- he can poke his ears full of toilet paper."

"I am sorry, buddy, you have been out-voted two to one," I informed him.

As I continued talking to the two men, the sleeping man pulled his blanket up over his head and cuddled up into a ball. He was determined not to hear any part of this message from this "Jesus Freak."

Perhaps I did talk a little louder, and after a few minutes, I noticed that the blanket had been lifted a little ways and I saw an ear sticking out.

A few minutes later, the blanket was thrown off, and he swung his feet over the edge of the bunk and onto the floor as he sat up. Soon he started asking questions, and within fifteen minutes he came up to the bars and got saved.

Before I left, Doug begged me to come back and see him again the next day, Monday. Even though he was now a child

110 / CALLING GOD'S TOWER...COME IN' PLEASE!

of God, he wanted to hear more about God's Word.

Doug said, "You just have to come to see me tomorrow, because Tuesday I am going to be sentenced to several years in Jackson prison, and they will take me the same day."

"I can't promise, Doug, but I will promise to try to see you. I have to fly to Indianapolis tonight and I won't get back until 4:30 a.m. Then I will have to see if a turn key will be available to allow me to visit you, but I will try."

"Please do," he begged, as I left the catwalk.

Returning from Indianapolis I went to a 7:00 a.m. prayer meeting, and then to the jail. Fortunately a turn key was available and I was able to take Doug to a private room and spent an hour with him going over the scriptures. Doug asked me to go to his home town and talk to his wife, Pat, about Jesus.

The next week, as I was driving to a speaking engagement, I left early and went through Doug's home town.

On the way, I prayed to God that if He wanted me to talk to Pat, she would be home, and if He didn't want me to talk to her, He would not have her at home. I drove in the driveway and got out of the car. I noticed a young lady walking across a lawn to another house carrying a small boy, accompanied by a little girl and an elderly lady.

I immediately went up to the young lady, and shook her hand and said, "I am Coach Eby, and I'll bet you are Pat, and you are carrying your son, Dale, and this pretty little girl is Mary Ann, but I don't know this other lady."

Pat seemed astounded, but pleased that I knew all their names. She replied, "This lady is my mother-in-law, Doug's mother, and Doug has told us about you."

After meeting Doug's father, I asked Pat if she would like to have me come into her house and talk to her. She agreed. Pat listened carefully as I gave her two Bibles, and talked to her about this new way of life that God had given Doug, and now would give her if she would accept Jesus. As we went through the scriptures with Pat reading the verses, while I explained them to her, she cried with tears of joy as our merciful Lord sent the Holy Spirit into her life, and she also joined the

Family of God.

I have received letters from Pat and from Doug, plus phone calls, and I have visited Pat. Later, I flew to Ionia to visit Doug who had been transferred to Ionia State Prison from Jackson. I praise God for the way He prepares individuals for the sowing of the seed.

Why Doesn't God Tell It As It Is?

I was speaking with Zeke in a private room at the county jail. Zeke was a black inmate from Ann Arbor. I could sense immediately that he had a "chip" on his shoulder.

"Why don't the Bible tell it as it is?" He asked.

"The Bible does," I replied.

Zeke countered, "Then why don't the Bible tell that Moses was black. I know he was; why don't the Bible say so."

"Listen, Zeke, I don't care if Moses was black, white, purple, green, or red; that is not the issue. The real issue is if you want to accept Jesus in faith and trust."

"You know the blacks have been mistreated, why don't you admit it," he poked at me.

"Don't throw that black and white 'jazz' at me, Zeke," I countered. "Do you know if you have the same type of blood as I have, that I can receive blood transfusions from you, and you from me without any harmful results? Listen, Zeke, just because the Lord, when He created you, saw fit to furnish you with more pigment in the middle layer of your epidermis, than He did me, don't try to make me feel guilty."

Zeke understood and that broke the barrier down.

However, Zeke would not join the Family of God. He believed in God, and even agreed that God wrote the Bible in the original writings, but he would not accept Jesus as the Son of God, or God upon the earth. I told Zeke it was his choice to believe this or not, but according to the scriptures, he could not become a child of God without believing that Jesus is the Son of God, and no way could he go to Heaven without believing this. Zeke is still outside the fold, and it still doesn't make any difference what his color is.

Hey, You!

One Sunday afternoon, I was visiting the jail in Grand Haven, Michigan. I walked along the catwalk until I came to a cell with two young men in it. One was lying on a top bunk and the other was on the other side of the cell, lying on a lower bunk reading a magazine. I spoke to the one on the upper bunk, and found that his name was George. I started telling George why I knew the Bible was true, and asked him if he would accept a testament from me as a gift. I put his name in it, and he reluctantly took it. I continued to talk about the Bible and Jesus, but he didn't seem to be too interested. I continued to tell George how God had entered my life, and how He had changed it into a real happy adventure, and George was now listening intently. However, the other man named Lowell -- as I found out later -- kept reading his magazine, and seemed as though he could care less about what we were talking about. As I continued to talk with George, I kept glancing across the cell at Lowell out of the corner of my eye. Every time I glanced his way, I saw his great big eyes staring at me over the top of that magazine. I threw a testament through the bars at him, and at the same time hollered, "Hey you, catch." He dropped the magazine, and caught the testament. Within a matter of thirty minutes both George and Lowell joined the Family of God and accepted Jesus as their personal Saviour. How I praise God for the power of His Written Word!

So shall my word be that goeth forth out of my mouth; it shall not return unto me void, but it shall accomplish that which I please, and it shall prosper in the thing whereto I sent it.
Isaiah 55:11

GOD IS IN THE SERVICE

Now Is The Acceptable Time

"Coach, another fellow wants to see you before you leave," the turn key at the county jail notified me.

"Bring him in now," I answered. "Don and I are now through talking."

The turn key brought in a young man by the name of Lee. In about forty minutes I had gone through the scriptures with Lee, and he had professed the necessary steps to join the Family of God.

After closing in prayer, I asked Lee why he had asked for me.

"Five years ago I was being inducted into the Army to leave for Vietnam," he said. "You came down at six a. m. and gave each one of us a small black testament, and also prayed for us. To tell the truth, I didn't want that Bible, and I didn't want to be prayed for. In fact, as soon as you left I threw the Bible away. But, you know all the time I was in the Army and ever since, I have been unable to forget that prayer, and the fact I threw that Bible away. Then when I was thrown into jail, I knew I needed something. And so I asked for you."

Isn't God marvelous? I personally would have been discouraged and might have given up on Lee if I had known he had thrown that Bible away. But not God. He sowed the seed five years ago, and five years later at the acceptable time, He brought this young man into the Family of God. Isn't He wonderful? After being saved, Lee was given a two year stretch in Jackson prison. After being released, Lee still had the dope and many other problems. Recently he has started reading the Bible and attending Bible studies, and Our Lord is now helping him with his problems. Praise God for His patience and persistence!

God Cannot Be Limited

Back in 1949, Coldwater High School won the state championship in basketball. I was fortunate to be the head coach at that time. On this team I had a center by the name of Roy, a six foot, one inch, large boned boy from the country. Roy was an outstanding high shcool athlctc especially in basketball and football, but he wasn't much interested in spiritual things. I rarely could get him to church, but now and then he would come to Sunday School. I thought to myself, what an influence Roy would have on the young people in our community if he would become a Christian. I concluded that Roy just wasn't the type to be interested in spiritual things. Did you every try to limit God's Power?

After graduating from Coldwater High School as an outstanding athlete in all sports, Roy joined the United States Navy to serve a hitch for his country. Upon being inducted, he received a Bible, and while overseas he started reading the Bible. Eventually, Roy came face to face with Jesus, and accepted Him as personal Saviour. About eight years ago, Roy, a guest minister from California, was preaching from the pulpit of one of the largest churches in Coldwater. The local paper had a pre-Sunday story on the front page with Roy's picture. According to the story, a former all-star athlete would be preaching in this church that Sunday. The church was packed. There was not room for all to sit down. Many were standing in the aisles and in the back of the church.

Did the people come to hear the Gospel? I am afraid not. I believe that many came because they didn't believe anything could change Roy into a preacher.

But God's Word could---and did.

I sat in the very front pew and listened to my former all-star athlete tell how reading God's Word changed his life completely. Also how it could change the life of all his friends out in front of him, if only they would read it, believe it, and receive it unto themselves in faith and trust in Jesus Christ.

I receive Roy's monthly church news letter and God is blessing his ministry. I praise the Lord for a God that cannot be limited, who can change the life of anyone and everyone who is willing to turn his life over to Him.

"I Will Tell Him Off"

After speaking in a church service in Cheboygan, Michigan, I went to the back of the church to greet the people as they left the sanctuary. A young lady came up to me and said, "I am mad." I asked her what her name was, and she informed me, Dana. I asked, "What are you mad about, Dana?" "I am mad at my husband," she replied. "I told him that we were having a special speaker at the church, and tried to get him to come but he wouldn't. I believe if he had been here, the Lord would have touched his heart."

"What is wrong with your husband," I asked.

Dana exploded, "He is anti-church, anti-preacher, anti-Bible, anti-God, anti-wife, anti-children, and anti-Christian."

"I would be happy to come over and visit him this afternoon on one condition," I offered.

"What's that," Dana wanted to know.

"That your husband invites me over to talk with him" I insisted. "You know where I am eating Sunday dinner. After you talk with your husband, George, if he doesn't want to see me, you call me, but if I don't hear from you I will be over at 4:00 p.m."

As I was eating dinner, the phone rang. I told Peggy, my hostess, that undoubtedly Dana was calling to tell me that George didn't want to see me. Peggy answered the phone. It was Dana, who related the following to Peggy who passed it on to me. "I came home from church and told George that the special speaker at the church was coming over to talk to him. He exploded. He told me to tell that crazy religious nut to stay away from here. He said it was bad enough to have you push that other preacher onto me and your other friends, and bad enough to live with you, without having another fanatic preaching at me. Then I told him I would have to call and tell him not to come, as that was the agreement. But he then hollered,"Don't call him. Let him come and I will tell him off to his face. So, Peggy, tell Mr. Eby that he shouldn't come."

I told Peggy to tell Dana I would be there as long as George said I could come.

After Peggy hung up, her husband Ray said, "I am a good friend of George's, and I had better go with you."

I told Ray to stay at home. I didn't want to take him with me. I wanted to take God with me, someone who has great power and is really able.

We had just finished eating when Dana arrived. She had driven over to try to talk me out of seeing George.

"Mr. Eby, he is really in an ugly mood and is ready to tell you off. It just doesn't make sense for you to go over at this time," Dana begged.

I again asked Dana if George said I couldn't come, and she said, "No, he wants you to come so he can tell you off."

I insisted that I was going, and asked her to take me over to her house. So she drove me over, took me in the house, and pointed George out to me; then she ran out of the house and jumped in her car and took off.

George was sitting in a large easy chair next to the

television, smoking a cigarette. I rushed over to him and grabbed his hand and shook it. "I am sure glad to meet you, George. I am Floyd Eby from Coldwater, and it sure is good to meet another old Navy swab."

George was in command of the Coast Guard station at Cheboygan.

I started telling him about some funny Coast Guard and Navy jokes and in just a few minutes he was laughing.

Eight minutes later, I was talking to him about the Bible and Jesus.

Twenty minutes later, George had professed the necessary steps to join the Family of God and accepted Jesus as Saviour.

I just know God had him prepared, and it was real with him. He asked me if I was going to speak at the church that night, and I assured him that I was. The next question from George was quite funny.

"Are you going to tell those Christians off?"

I assured him that I was going to speak from God's Word. You see, it was hard for George to identify himself with Christians, because of his long-standing, deep hangups about churches, Christians and preachers.

George drove me back over to Ray and Peggy's home, where his wife Dana was also. We ate an evening lunch, had a good time of Christian fellowship, then we all went to church together. After the message at the church, I had another fine talk with George. He was concerned about me flying my plane all the way home to Coldwater so late at night and with only one motor. I assured George that one motor plus God was much better than two motors without God, but he still thought that at night I should have two motors, plus God.

George and Dana and their three beautiful children were still having trouble, and the marriage was on thin ice. Although being a Christian, George still had many hangups on preachers, churches, and their traditional views on all the do's and don'ts. I kept writing both of them and calling to encourage each one to read the Bible, talk with God, be with other Christians, and to serve Jesus. I also reminded Dana to pray for George, also to get as close to God herself as she possibly could, and not to push or nag George.

One night when I telephoned, George answered, and I asked him how he and his family were. "Just great," he answered. "I am now really praising the Lord. I have joined a church, I'm teaching a Sunday School class, and also helping promote a new building addition."

Dana also came to the phone. "Floyd, I just can't believe it. God has worked miracles. I have to pinch myself to make sure this is not just a dream. Things have changed completely, and we are praising God every day."

What a wonderful Saviour we have who can make family life worth living.

A Stormy Conversion

My overseas duty in the Navy, and particularly during a typhoon had so much to do with my conversion, spiritual start, and covenant with God. I wish to tell you about my experiences in this particular typhoon which was such an eventful incident in my Christian life.

Two days out of Okinawa enroute to Leyte Gulf we hit some rough weather. Knowing that we were in the typhoon area during the typhoon season, I kept a close check on all the weather reports coming in. As soon as the coding board had weather reports broken I would take them to the Navigator's shack and chart the direction that the different storms were traveling.

It looked like we were definitely heading for trouble.

The weather reports and charts indicated we had no way out of the storm short of turning back to Okinawa. I knew the "old man" would not do that. Fortunately, we were sailing by ourselves and had no one else to look out for. During real rough weather, the stewards generally put a cover on the wardroom table that had holes in it. This wooden cover was used to set the dishes on so they could not slide around on the table or onto the deck, and it was clamped to the table which in turn was solidly fastened to the deck. However, that night for supper, the stewards had not seen the necessity of putting

the cover on, because up to that time it had not been too bad.
We stood, all the officers off watch, around the table
waiting for the Captain to come in. This was normal
procedure. When meals were ready to be served, a steward
notified the Captain. The officers would rise when the
Captain entered the room, and then everyone would sit down
together. Very seldom was an officer late to a meal unless he
was on watch. If any officer did come in late, he would
apologize to the Captain as he took his seat. The rolling of the
ship was becoming worse by the minute.

The bowls of soup had just been served when the ship took a
sudden lurch to the port throwing the "old man" back over
onto his back, and five servings of soup onto his lap. The
other soup went skittering onto the deck with the other
Officers.

"Willy," the "old man" shouted at the chief steward.
"Where is the top cover?" By now the "old Man" and the
other officers had regained their seats, and Willy was
struggling to his feet. "Answer up, Willy," the "old man"
shouted!

"I didn't think we all would need it, sir," Willy replied.

"When did you ever think you were going to use it? Just
before the ship capsized?" growled the Captain.

"Do you all want us to put it on now, sir?" inquired Willy.

"No, the damage has already been done. Pick up those
dishes and get us some more soup!"

It was funny to see all that soup go into the Captain's lap.
But no one had laughed. We didn't know it then but that was
the last meal we were to have for some time.

All that night the storm worsened and the sea and ship
rolled more and more. In the early morning hours the
typhoon struck its peak.

We now understood how helpless we really were against
God's nature. Waves were sixty feet high with foam boiling at
each top. The waves were tossing the ship around like a
matchstick.

The ship would strike the trough between two waves and
then start up the next wave, and the wave would try to bash

through the ship. Although the bridge was at the highest point of the superstructure, solid water would strike the glass shield and spray would fly all over the bridge. On watch on the open bridge, we hung on to the bulkheads as the ship tossed and rolled. Salt from the spray made my eyes smart, and I would occasionally take my tongue and wipe it around my mouth which was caked with concentrated salt.

The waves were of such size and intensity that we did not dare to head directly into them. The weight of the thousands of tons of water bashing the ship head on, would soon break it in two, I thought. However, we did not dare to steer a course parallel to the waves, because the waves would certainly capsize the ship. The only course we dared to steer was one that took us into the waves in a quarterly direction. We hoped this would relieve enough pressure head on to keep the ship from separating, and still not produce enough roll to capsize the ship.

The head on pressure of the water would, with each wave, seem to stop the ship momentarily. Then as the ship started to move on, the water pressure would cause a tremendous groaning and shrieking of the expansion plates of the ship. Each time it would sound like the ship was coming directly apart at the middle. The gigantic steel mast that came up through the superstructure at the rear part of the bridge led straight up toward the sky for sixty feet. It contained many yardarms, lights, hoists, antennae, as well as several tons of radar antenna at the very top.

As the bow of the ship started into and over the next wave, the head-on pressure of the water made this gigantic steel mast, sixteen inches in diameter, shake and vibrate all the way to the top.

The tons of radar antenna shook the top of the mast like the tail of a setter when it located a bird. We watched the antenna until it vibrated to a stop. Then would wait until the next wave and look again to see if the mast was going to shake the antenna off and onto our heads.

Our ship was built to normally withstand sixty degrees of roll. When a ship is upright in the ocean, the mast forms a ninety degree angle with the level of the water. Sixty degrees meant that the ship could roll up to two thirds of the way over without capsizing. As Bud said jokingly, at that time we should now be getting sub pay, sea pay, and flight pay. We were now spending one third of our time under water, one third on top of the water, and the other one third in the air above the water.

I kept checking the list, and we were consistently rolling over sixty degrees.

Once I checked it when it read sixty-six degrees.

As we started into a wave the ship would start rolling either to the starboard or to the port. It would go over as far as the wave rolled it. Then it would tremble several times like it was making up its mind whether to come back or go on over. It would then start up-right again, and repeat the same procedure to the other side.

I had to shout to make it possible for anyone to hear me due to the great amount of noise caused by the storm, mainly the high velocity wind screeching through the wires and superstructure.

No one dared to venture out onto the main deck---even to lash down gear---without having a large line tied around his middle to prevent him from being washed overboard by the overwhelming waves.

Soon, 215 officers and men out of the 224 experienced seamen were deathly sea sick. Only those who were so sick they couldn't get out of the sack were relieved of their duty, because someone had to stand the watches. The only way to describe sea sickness is that the seasick person wishes he was dead, and generally prays to the Lord to strike him dead. I was one of the fortunate few who did not get seasick. When you are sick, you can hardly force yourself to think of food, let alone eat it. However, that is when you wish that you could die, when you have to vomit and there is nothing left in your stomach to vomit. You gag and heave until all food is emptied out of your stomach. Then you keep right on gagging and heaving until blood starts coming up, and it seems like your insides are coming right up out of your stomach and out of your throat.

Even if anyone had wanted to eat, they would have had to get their own food. All the stewards and cooks were deathly sick. I kept some slices of bread in my pocket. Although thoughts of any food, including bread, were distasteful, I forced myself to chew and swallow some of this bread every so often, so I would be sure to keep something in my stomach. I believe this kept me from being seasick.

I was standing four hours on watch and four off now, due to the fact that a number of the officers were unable to stand their watches. I spent most of the four hours off watch in the radio shack. I had four radio operators covering four different frequencies, a radio supervisor, and a file clerk. The operators were sitting in chairs anchored to holes in the deck, earphones on, typing the morse code groups on message blanks. Around each chair and each operator I had a large rope; the rope hooked to the bulkhead, then around the chair and operator, and again hooked to the bulkhead on the other side. This prevented the chair and operator from lurching over and falling.

In between each two operators, I had a bucket secured to the bulkhead for the operators to vomit in. These operators were gagging and heaving until nearly all of them were vomiting blood. Quite frequently one of them would gag and heave so much he would finally pass out. I would then immediately unhook the rope, and drag him out onto the deck. I would drag another sick but conscious man into the chair, hook him in with the rope, put the earphones on him and tell him to get to work. By the time another passed out, one of the other two that were not on the earphones would be conscious again.

Forcing really sick men like this to work was one of the hardest things that I had to do all during the time I was in the service. Most of these boys had been out of high school only a short time. I hated to be the monster that I now had to be, because the frequencies had to be covered. The safety of the whole ship and all of its men depended on it.

In all of our previous sea duty, I had never seen the crew

GOD IS IN THE SERVICE / 123

and officers as scared as they now appeared. I know I was scared, and I am sure they were too.

Against the enemy we knew what to do. Against a typhoon of this type there wasn't much we could do.

I know I felt helpless, and I think the rest of the crew did too. A number of the boys in my department who were still in their teens would ask, "Sir, do you think the ship will capsize?" "Mr. Eby, do you believe the ship will break in two?" "Sir, do you think the ship will last the night out?"

I would say, "Don't worry boys, this ship will ride this breeze through with no trouble. You can't capsize one of these Destroyer Escorts. This ship will take more roll and pounding than any other ship in the Navy. These DE's are really built. They will stand almost anything!"

This not only made the boys feel better, but it also made me feel more optimistic.

My chief radioman who had been to sea for eighteen years pulled me into the transmitter shack.

"Sir, are you believing that crap you are handing out? If you are, you are crazy. I have been to sea for eighteen years. I also know how these tubs are built, and I also know that this ship will not last the night out!"

"I don't believe it will either chief," I said, "But I am not going to tell those kids that."

"Oh, I see what you are up to now, Sir," he replied as he waddled out to take care of one of the boys who had passed out.

Night was terrible! Darkness seemed to bring with it added fear and helplessness. I was spending most of my time either on the bridge or in the radio shack. I was relieved for four hours and went to my stateroom to try and get some rest. I laid in my sack with my clothes on, holding on to keep from rolling out of the upper bunk. My wife's and daughter's picture was bounding all over the room. I put it away into a cabinet, and let my thoughts dwell on my family for a few minutes.

In a way it was sort of comforting, even though I was convinced I would never see them again.

What a way to pass out of this life! Never get a scratch from enemy action but become missing in action because of wind! It was impossible to sleep for two reasons. If you fell asleep, you would let go of the side of the bed, and roll out and fall onto the deck. So I continually held on and rolled with the ship. The ship would hit a trough and roll over to the starboard side some sixty degrees. Then it would start to tremble and shake, trying to make up its mind whether to continue on over and capsize or start on its way back upright.

Every time it trembled, I prayed. "Dear Lord, please bring it back again, back, back, back. Thank you Lord, it's coming back." Then I would have around six seconds to rest before the ship would be sixty degrees to the port, starting to tremble and shake. "Oh, God, bring her back once more; come on baby, come back. Thank you Lord, she is coming back again." Six seconds more of rest and the whole procedure over again. We all knew that once the ship kept going and capsized we would all be dead in a matter of minutes. Nearly everyone on board the ship was praying but for different results. Some were praying like I was to bring the ship safely through the storm. Those who were deathly seasick were praying to God to capsize the ship in order to get them out of their misery. "Oh, merciful God, please roll the thing clear over so I may now rest in peace!"

My stateroom door opened and Jay, my roommate, poked his head in and shouted at me.

"Hey you, Eby. Several five inch shells have broken loose in the forward handling room, and are bounding from bulkhead to bulkhead. If one of them goes off, it will set all our ammo off and blow us clear to Heaven."

"For Pete's sake, Jay, get a working party down there and lash them secure, before those shells do go off."

"Don't get up tight Eby, I have already taken care of that detail. I just wanted to see if I could scare you."

"Forget it, Jay, there is a limit to how scared you can be, and I reached that limit hours ago!"

Jay left for the bridge. About two hours later some of the electrical wiring that had been pulled loose by the straining of the ship started an electrical fire right next to that same ammunition room. If it hadn't been for the alertness and presence of mind of my radio technician, Jerry, it would have exploded the ammo and our troubles would have been over. However, Jerry was close by when it started and quickly grabbed the extinguishers and sand and put it out. Praise God for Jerry!

Just before I went back on watch, I was talking to Ron, the Navigator and Executive Officer in the wardroom. He was sick, but he had dragged himself out of the sack to go to the head. He had seen me in the wardroom and wondered how things were going. Bud came into the wardroom and said he thought the "old man" would soon abandon the old tub because the storm was becoming worse.

"What good would that do," I asked. "No one could live in this sea on a life raft. A person couldn't even stick to a raft for two minutes before a wave would tear him off. Even if you could stick to the raft, what would you do, jumping sixty feet up and then immediately sixty feet down."

"I know it," Bud replied. "But if this storm gets any worse, we know the ship will capsize, and do you want to go down with it without attempting to save your life?"

"No," I answered. "I'm not that sick yet, but let's face it, either the ship will kill us or save us, and there is no other help for us except God Almighty."

Bud was an atheist, and would argue anytime that God's name was mentioned.

"You still think the God in your fairy tale is going to save you?" he asked.

"When this tub starts to capsize, you will have to at least admit to me on our way down that there is no such God."

"Bud," I exclaimed, "You have your belief and I have mine. But when this ship goes down, you will surely continue on your way down, and I know that I will start back on the upward way."

Ron changed the subject, "Has anyone seen Saari?"

John Saari was a first division officer, and his quarters were in after-officers' quarters.

"I haven't seen John since this storm started," I said.
"He is sicker than a goose back in the quarters," Bud stated.
"I guess I will go back and see how he is coming before I go on watch," I replied.

I made my way back to after-officers' quarters, and found John lying on his lower berth. He looked pale and peaked and about ready to die. He had been vomiting up blood, and was tossing in agony.

"John," I said, "I believe you had better get up to the wardroom because the storm is getting worse by the minute. It is a possibility that the 'old man' may abandon ship. It looks like it is bound to roll over and capsize."

John started raving, "I hope the tub does roll over, the sooner, the better, and I am not going to move, because the sooner it does, the sooner I will be out of my misery. I will sing Praise God from whom all blessings flow on our way down, because the Lord will be doing me a great favor if He will capsize this ship immediately."

John continued to rave, and I left as I knew there was no way for me to help him. I didn't want to listen to him. I wanted to live.

I climbed up to the bridge and relieved the watch, and Conter was my JOD. It appeared as though the storm was worse than it was on my last watch, and the increased wind velocity, and the roll and pitch of the ship seemed to verify the fact.

I had been on watch only about thirty minutes when the "old man" came up the ladder. He went into the Navigator's shack, and looked at the weather reports and our dead reckoning position on the chart. He then pulled himself through the hatch onto the open bridge, and turned around just in time to get smacked in the face with part of a wave. It almost knocked him down but he held on to the bulkhead with one hand, and wiped his face with the sleeve of his other arm. He took a look dead ahead, and then made a tour around the bridge, traveling by means of pulling himself along with his arms hanging onto the bulkhead. By this time he had seen enough and said to me, "Kind of a heavy sea, isn't it?"

And with this bright statement completed, he waddled back down to his stateroom.

Conter asked, "Why don't the 'old man' do something? It looks like to me that we could possibly get out of this typhoon by changing course."

"I agree with you," I answered. "According to the storm reports of how this typhoon is traveling, about three degrees course change to the port would appear to take us out of this storm soon. But I suppose the 'old man' thinks that even this much change in course may cause enough more roll to capsize us."

"Horse Feathers!" Conter answered. "We plenty well know that if we don't get out of this storm soon this tub will break up. I say we ought to take the chance on the roll. It's the only chance we have."

One hour later the ship's roll was consistently registering in the high sixties, and the pitch of the ship was worse. I called the "old man" on the phone.

"Captain, this is the Officer of the Deck. The storm seems to be getting worse all the time, and I don't believe the ship will take much more."

"Well, what do you expect me to do about it?" He hung up.

Ten minutes later I called him again. "Captain, this is the OOD. According to the latest weather reports, and our dead reckoning position, I believe we would improve our situation by changing our course to the port by three degrees."

"Forget it." The click sounded in my ears as the Captain hung up his receiver.

"Sir," One of the men yelled at me, "Forward repair party reports that Compartment 204A is filling up with water...faster than they can pump it out. One of their pumps has crapped out."

I called the Captain. "Captain, this is the OOD. Compartment 204A is filling up with water."

"Pump it out," he yelled. And 'click' went the receiver.

I called again, "Captain, they are pumping it out, but it is filling up faster than they can pump it, because one of the pumps is broken."

"Fix it." Click went the receiver as he hung up again. I was mad.

"Talker, tell the forward repair party to fix their pump, and pump that compartment out. I want that compartment emptied of water, and I don't care how it's done, even if they have to do it with a couple of buckets. Tell them to get on the ball and get their job done."

The bridge talker relayed the message word for word, and I heard no more from Compartment 204A.

As soon as I was relieved from watch, I hurried down to the radio shack to see how the men were holding up. In order to reach the main radio shack, I passed the Captain's Cabin. I believe all the men and officers were scared like me. But I didn't believe the Captain would be scared of anything. I believed he must have had ice water running through his veins for blood.

As I started to go into the radio shack, I looked at the Captain's Cabin. The Captain had his door lashed open so he could get out in a hurry if he suddenly needed to do so. Through his open doorway, I saw the "old man" lying down on his sack. Amid the pitching, rolling and groaning of the ship, the Captain was quietly lying on his sack. He was holding onto the bunk with one hand to keep from falling off, and in the other hand he held a book which he was reading.

I looked at the book, and read the title, "The Life of Benjamin Franklin."

Forget Ben Franklin, I thought. The Captain had better be reading the Bible, or a book entitled, "How to Navigate Ships Through Typhoons."

We were in the typhoon for two entire days and three whole nights. It seemed like two hundred years. Then came the morning when the typhoon had spent itself, and the fury was gone. The sea was still rough, but the waves were down to about thirty feet. It seemed like we were walking on solid ground compared to what we had just experienced. Each hour the sea got better. Everyone began to look better, and started to yell for food. Even John came up to the wardroom and we were now only about fifty short miles from Leyte Gulf. The crew and officers by now had had two good meals and everyone seemed to be as happy as birds. I went into the radio shack to check on things. As I looked around, an urgent message came over CW, designated action to our ship and to the "old man."

I took the dispatch, chased the coding board watch out of the coding room, and broke the message in privacy. It was a good thing I did it in privacy. It was orders from ComPhilSeaFron, ordering the "old man" to take the ship back into the typhoon, locate and rescue two ocean-going tugs. The tugs were in distress in the same typhoon we had just passed through.

I guarded the message secretly. I knew that if the word got around, some of the boys might start jumping overboard. I knew that if one man found out the contents of the message, the whole ship would soon know.

I took the message to the Captain, and after reading it, he asked, "Did anyone else see this message?"

"No, Sir," I answered.

"Who broke it?" he inquired.

"I did, Sir."

"Send me the Navigator," he ordered. "And tell no one about the contents of this message."

"Aye, Aye, Sir."

We soon made a complete turn about, but fortunately nobody knew why. However, when we arrived in the typhoon area, the typhoon had spent itself and moved on. We searched for the tugs for two days and then received orders to give up the search. We then proceeded to Leyte Gulf without mishap.

During this typhoon, I decided once and for all to put my faith in Jesus Christ, and accept Him as my personal Saviour, and join the Family of God. While our entire crew was right next to death during this typhoon experience, we had 224 praying Christians. After we sailed out into smooth seas and the wind had calmed down, I would guess that we only had about a dozen Christians left.

No, the others didn't fall overboard, but they no longer

needed God.

I personally covenanted with My God that if He would bring me through the typhoon and certain death, I would serve Him forever. However, after the war, I became too busy doing the things that I wanted to do, and I forgot my covenant with God.

Even though I was surely a child of God, I did not see the need to discipline myself to come close to God and live for Him. Therefore, my Christianity didn't become a real, vital, vibrant, dominate, and happy part of my life until later.

*And to know the love of Christ, which
passeth knowledge, that ye might be filled
with all the fullness of God.
Ephesians 3:19*

10

GOD GOES TO SCHOOL

What Are You Doing Here?

I traveled over to a nearby Michigan Gideon Camp to help them distribute New Testaments on one of their college campuses. We met for prayer first, at one of the Gideon's nearby homes.

One of the Gideons brought in a copy of the college newspaper and threw it on the table in front of me and said, "What do you think of that, Floyd?"

I picked up the paper and started reading the article written by a male student writer. The article included some of the filthiest language I had seen in print. It was so bad it made me sick to read it. I told the Gideon, "I believe we should pray that our Lord will not allow this writer to be used of the devil to block our distribution of the Bible at this college."

We had only been on the campus for a short time when a young lady came up to me and asked, "What are you doing here? I am Marian, the editor of the college newspaper, and I want to know what is going on?"

I replied, "Where do you want to discuss it, Marian?"

"We will go up in the journalism room," she notified me.

"Great," I said, "Lead away and I will follow."

So Marian took me up to the journalism room where two boys and one girl writer were present. I sat down and Marian spoke up, "Now, we want to know what you are doing?"

"It is simple, Marian, I answered. "We are handing out free copies of the Bible to anyone who wishes to take one, and the price is right, isn't that great?"

"That isn't what I mean," Marian said. "I want to know why you are doing it?"

"I am sure glad that you asked that question, Marian," I retaliated, "Because I want you to know the real reason."

So I proceeded, in the next forty minutes, to tell the four of them about God's Wonderful Plan for their lives. The whiplash, in the form of anti-God and anti-Bible questions and comments was severe.

Finally, Marian spoke up. "I can't buy that Heaven and Hell you are talking about after death." Marian continued, "If there is any Heaven or Hell, it is right here while we are on this earth, and depends on how we treat our fellowmen."

"Where ever did you get that idea, Marian?" I asked.

"I want you to know, Sir, that it is my own personal opinion."

"I just knew that, Marian," I countered. "I also know, Marian, that your personal opinion is only a little more valuable than Floyd Eby's, and mine is absolutely worthless. You have to go to God's Word to get the truth."

Marian and her three companions at this time had to go to class. I went back into the lobby and continued to hand out New Testaments.

One hour later, Marian came back from class, and accosted me, "Mr. Eby, I am going to the Dean, and see if I can have you come over and speak to the entire student body at noon hour."

"Great, Marian, I would like that. And the price will be right," I answered.

Two days later I called Marian at the college and she said,

"Mr. Eby, I went to the Dean and requested you as a noon hour speaker at our regular gathering. I couldn't get you in, because the Dean said we had exams next week and it was too near to the end of the school year to take a chance of upsetting the applecart."

"That is O.K., Marian," I answered. "But you know, Marian, I would like to come over and meet with you personally, because you have some questions that have not yet been answered. What about it?"

Marian made arrangements to meet me three days later at noon, so that day I drove over to the college before I continued on to Detroit for a speaking engagement. I told Marian I would meet her at noon, but forgot to agree on a location. All the way over, I kept thinking Marian would certainly "cop" out. Those male writers would tell her to forget it. The further I drove, the more I was convinced that I was wasting time and mileage. Then I thought, Lord, that is your job. If you want me to talk to her, you will have her there. If she isn't there, I will know you don't want me to talk with Marian.

At 11:55 a.m., I climbed the steps to the large lobby on the second floor, and hopefully waited for Marian to come along. While I was standing there, the Dean came out with the President and introduced me. The President said, "You must like it here, you are back again. But what for?"

"I came back to meet with Marian, the editor of your college newspaper," I answered.

Immediately the President and the Dean were on the defensive, because they had received many complaints about the language of their newpaper, especially from the area ministers.

"We have had trouble with that paper and staff," the President defended.

"I am sure you have, but do you know why, Mr. President? It is because only God changes people, and your rules and regulations will not have much effect on that staff."

I started witnessing to the President and the Dean, and the Dean spoke up. "I will go get Marian for you, Floyd."

I think the Dean wanted to get away from there. He soon

brought Marian back.

Marian led me to the student union where students were eating lunch, and we sat at a vacant table near the windows. I presented her with a personal Worker's Testament with her name in it, and several verses underlined.

As Marian would read the verse, I would discuss it with her. Forty-five minutes later, Marian accepted Jesus as her Personal Saviour, joined the Family of God, and signed the back cover indicating her important decision.

Before Marian transferred colleges, I had the opportunity to visit with her and correspond with her.

Friends, legislation and rules will not stop the unbelievers and their un-Godly way of living. But God can change their lives.

A few months later, this same Dean was presented a dignitary Bible at a banquet. He responded that his daughter had become a Christian, and now for the first time, the Bible meant a great deal to him personally. Praise God for His Word that is sharper than any two-edged sword.

No, Thank You, I Am An Atheist

On October 30, 1974, God chose seventy-seven Gideon Missionaries of Michigan churches, who took time off their jobs to hand out over 12,000 copies of the Bible to over twelve thousand students at Western Michigan University at Kalamazoo, Michigan. I was fortunate to be one of the seventy-seven.

As I was handing out New Testaments, I was barking up trade, "Get your free Bible today; get it now before the price goes up. The price is right; they are going like hotcakes, get yours before we run out...this is the greatest bargain ever." A young lady approached me, and I hollered, "Don't you want your free Bible now, young lady?"

She answered, "No thank you, I am an atheist," and she walked on by.

I shouted at her as she left, "Well, have a good day, anyway."

Five minutes later, she returned and approaching me said, "I would like one of those Bibles."

"Certainly," I replied, "But aren't you the young atheist that just turned one down a few minutes ago?"

"Yes, I am. But I am not so sure anymore," she said softly.

"Where are you going now, friend?" I wanted to know.

"I am going to class at 12:00," she answered.

"It is 11:35 now," I said. "What are you doing until twelve?"

"Nothing," she replied.

"Wouldn't you like to go over to that bench with me, and let me tell you about the Bible and Jesus?" I inquired.

"I would like that," she said.

So, this young co-ed and I went over and sat down on the bench. I presented her with a personal worker's testament with her name in it. I showed her through the salvation verses, and after she read each verse out loud, I would tell her about God's Wonderful Plan for her life. Just twenty minutes later, she read the back cover out loud, "My Decision to Receive Christ as My Saviour, Confessing to God that I am a sinner, and believing that the Lord Jesus Christ died for my sins on the cross and was raised for my justification, I do now receive and confess Him as my personal Saviour." Then Barbara signed her name as a Child of God, a former atheist from Detroit, Michigan, but now one of His chosen.

As I visit and correspond with Barbara, she tells me how she is reading the Bible, and how she has been attending campus crusade. Campus Crusade has been helping her to read and understand God's Word.

I didn't tell Barbara that I had given her name to several different members of Campus Crusade, just to make sure someone invited her into the fellowship of believers.

50 Romeo

One night at midnight, I was flying my plane out of the Kent Airport at Grand Rapids, Michigan. I started the motor, and as you have to do at all controlled airports, I turned on my radio, and secured permission from the tower.

"Grand Rapids tower, this is Cessna 5750 Romeo, requesting permission to taxi to runway to depart for Coldwater, Michigan. Over."

The man in the airport tower came back with instructions, and I slowly taxied my plane toward the proper runway.

The tower operator interrupted, "50 Romeo, do you live in Coldwater?"

You are only to use proper terminology and only for flight and taxi business, or you can lose your license.

I replied, "50 Romeo, affirmative."

"Do you know anything about the Catholic Church in Coldwater?"

"50 Romeo, affirmative."

"Do you know Father at the church?"

Once again I came back, "50 Romeo, affirmative."

You see, I didn't want to lose my license, and I was now speeding down the runway for takeoff.

Back came the tower operator, "Would you please call him when you get home and tell him Jay said, 'Hello.' Father drove all the way up here to encourage us to have a weekly prayer meeting."

I was airborne, heading away from Grand Rapids, but when the tower operator mentioned a weekly prayer meeting, I forgot all about regulations and shouted in the mike, "Praise God, I am President of the Michigan Gideons and I am glad to hear you are having prayer meetings."

"You are a Gideon?" he inquired.

"Yes," I said.

"You know what?" he asked.

"What?"

He answered, "My boy brought home a little red book from the Catholic school the other day." He didn't call it a Bible or a testament, but just a little red book. "You know I have been reading it, and it is a good book," he announced.

I shouted, "Amen" into the mike.

Jay asked, "Would you do something for me?"

"What is it, Jay?" I inquired.

"Would you come up in the tower and talk to me some time?" he asked.

By that time I was half way home, almost to Battle Creek.

"I will do that, Jay," I promised. Late one evening, a friend brought me to the Grand Rapids airport, so I could fly my plane home. The weather looked bad. I went up to the flight service weather station on the second deck, and asked them what the weather was like between Grand Rapids and Coidwater. He said, "Forget it, Buddy, it is terrible, and you aren't flying out of here tonight." I walked across the street and rented a motel room. I awoke the next morning after a good night's rest, and thought perhaps Jay would be home on his day off. I picked up the Grand Rapids phone book, and looked for Jay's telephone number.

There were two Jays with the same last name. I called the first one, and Jay answered.

"Is this the Jay that works in the Kent Airport tower?" I inquired.

"This is he," came the answer.

"Jay, this is Floyd Eby, the Gideon."

Jay's first three words were, "Praise the Lord!"

I talked with Jay on the phone for almost thirty minutes. I then said, "Jay, I have a very important question to ask you."

He said, "Shoot."

"Jay, just what is your personal relationship with the Lord Jesus Christ, now?" I asked.

He answered, "Floyd, I have gone to church all my life. It hasn't meant a thing to me until recently. Jesus came into my heart and my life and I am praising God every day."

I asked Jay how many they were having at weekly prayer meeting and he answered about five hundred.

You see, friends, you cannot bound the Word of God, but as God has promised, if His Word is put out, it will not return void.

I have never met Jay personally, but whether I do or not, I know I will meet him in Heaven.

Last winter, I was flying home from Traverse City and thirty miles northwest of Grand Rapids, I flew into a bad snowstorm. I was forced down to an unsafe altitude. I called Grand Rapids and asked for permission to squawk my transponder and go on radar. The radar operator kept giving me helpful information all the way past Grand Rapids, until I was ten miles north of the Allegan airport.

As he terminated the radar services, he also asked, "50 Romeo, how is the Bible business?"

"Is this Jay?" I wanted to know. And he affirmed it was. Many times Jay has given me special help in flying my plane through the Grand Rapids area. Doesn't God work in marvelous ways? I have never seen Jay, but I love him as I know he is my brother in Christ!

Are You A Jew?

"Young lady, would you like a free Bible?" I asked a girl on a college campus?

"No, thank you," she said, and walked on by.

Some time later, I thought the same girl walked by again, but I wasn't sure, so I asked her the same question again. She edged up real close to me, and leaned over to me and spoke into my ear, "Are you a Jew?"

I answered her with the same answer that I use every time someone asks me a question pertaining to races or denominations, or different religions.

"I am a believer."

She stuck out her hand, palm up, and said, "Put one there," and I placed a testament in her hand.

However, she didn't seem anxious to leave, and I started chatting with her about her interests and training. Her name was Doris and she informed me she was not living with her parents because she couldn't get along with them. I asked Doris her age and she said she was nineteen. I told her, "Doris, that means you are an adult, right?"

She agreed.

"I believe your parents are also adults, right?"

Once again she agreed.

GOD GOES TO SCHOOL / 139

"Doris, I have news for you. Only God changes adults, and that means only God can change your parents, and only God can change you." I continued, "I have a way of life that can't be beat. Would you like to hear about it? It is terrific and the price is right."

Doris and I went over and sat down in the lobby. I took out God's Word and told her about His way of life for Doris. As she read the verses and we discussed them, we prayed together after she had accepted Christ and joined the Family of God. What a wonderful Saviour we have.

The Old Schoolhouse

One day during my travels, I stopped at an old schoolhouse that had been converted into a home.

After introducing myself, I was invited in, and I chatted with the two parents and the three children. I told mom and dad that they undoubtedly had the best educated children in the area, because their children spent every night and all night at the schoolhouse.

A few minutes later, I left without saying a word about Jesus, because I had not felt God's leading.

A week later, I stopped again and made friends. The oldest child was Mabel, a tenth grader, and Hal and Lisa were of grade school age. The father was a huge, tough-talking man. The mother was more gracious.

The next week, I felt led of the Lord to talk to Mabel by herself. I asked her parents if Mabel and I could go into the kitchen and talk. I told them I had some good news to tell her.

Because I had established a friendship with the whole household by this time, everyone was agreeable. I took Mabel into the kitchen, gave her two Bibles and told her about Jesus. She accepted Jesus in about thirty-five minutes and joined tha Family of God. She was real pleased that she now understood and was really a Child of God. The next week, I asked Mabel, privately, what was the spiritual status of her parents. She told me that her mother was just like she, herself, had been; she just talked a good game. Her father didn't do even that, and had no interest whatsoever in spiritual things. The following week, after much prayer, I felt led of the Lord to talk with mom and dad, Rachael and Howard.

It was with much doubt and apprehension that I walked into the old schoolhouse that afternoon, planning to talk to these two parents about Jesus.

I just knew that this big, boisterous, rough-talking man was going to boot me right out of that schoolhouse when I opened my mouth about Jesus.

In fact, I was prepared to leave quickly.

However, I gave them both two Bibles each as gifts, and started talking to mom and dad at the kitchen table about Jesus.

Within fifteen minutes, this big, rough, tough man that I was afraid of, broke down and cried, with big tears rolling down each cheek, as both parents came into the Family of God.

I just praise God that He can and does prepare hearts. The next week, Hal and Lisa insisted that they also be told about Jesus, and the two made the schoolhouse family, a complete family in Jesus Christ.

God Loves Teenagers

Recently, I was speaking in a junior high school of about one hundred students. As I talked to them about this wonderful new way of life, I told them if they were already Christians and knew for sure, I praised God for their important decision. However, I emphasized that if God had been talking to them during the message, and they were doubtful about their actual relationship with Jesus, and honestly wanted to get right with God, to come into the chemistry room after the message. Praise God, seventy teenagers came in and wanted to get right with God for sure. I spent an hour with them, going over the scriptures and explaining in simple language the needed steps to be taken to join the Family of God. All seventy of them professed to believe, and receive Jesus as their Saviour and joined the

Family of God. I then drove over to a senior high school and spoke to an assembly. Six students, after the message, came into the teachers' lounge and accepted Christ as Saviour. The next week, I mailed a King James New Testament, and a copy of the Living Bible to each one of the seventy-six, and also wrote each one a personal letter. Since then, I have called many on the telephone, and answered each one of the dozens of letters that I have received. Praise God for the freshness, frankness, and enthusiasm of teenagers with whom God is working.

Passing Inspection

I was speaking at an early morning prayer breakfast to several hundred people. After the message, a principal of a junior high school, who was at the meeting, came to me and asked me if I would speak to their students. I readily agreed. After the assembly, three eighth grade girls came up and wanted to talk with me. After receiving permission from the principal, I took Pam, Sara, and Janet into a room, opened up the scriptures, and each one made sure that they were in the Family of God. I followed up with the usual procedure. I gave each one of them two Bibles, wrote each one a personal letter, called each one on the phone, and answered each letter I received.

The girls knew that I was going to speak at a banquet in Muskegon in about two weeks, and Sara and Janet wanted to go. I had not met their parents, but the girls had in some way received permission to go with me.

I agreed to fly to Grand Haven, and pick up the girls and fly them to Muskegon with me. However, the wind velocity that day was in the forty to fifty miles per hour range, which made it too dangerous. I called one of the girls and made arrangements to pick them up at Sara's house with my car.

Arriving at the house, I met Sara's parents and Janet's mother, who had brought her over.

After a few minutes of conversation, the girls and I left for Muskegon and for the banquet location. The girls were supposed to direct me there, but through the incessant chatter, we became mixed up and lost. We eventually found the location just as the banquet meal was ready to be served. Sara and Janet really quieted down when they saw the large crowd. I walked the girls up to the speaker's table, and introduced them to the moderator. I asked if arrangements could be made so I could sit with Sara and Janet during the meal and fellowship. During the introductions, I introduced Sara and Janet as my sisters in Christ, and asked them to stand up, which they reluctantly did.

How quiet they were during the evening, until we were in the car and headed home.

Arriving at Sara's home, we found her parents gone. Her grandmother was baby sitting with the younger children. Janet called her home and asked her parents to pick her up. As I nearly always do in situations such as this, I asked the girls and the grandmother to sit down around the table. I gave each one a Bible, and proceeded to have a short Bible study, with each one taking turns reading and then discussing the verses. Just as we started, Janet's father walked in and I introduced myself. I asked him if he would like to get in on our Bible study, and he agreed. After the short study, we had a circle prayer. I asked our Lord's blessing on all my new friends, and I left for home.

On the way to Muskegon, I had asked the girls how they had gotten permission to go with me...a stranger to all their parents?

The girls told me that all four parents had agreed that they were going to bring the girls to the airport. Then they were to give me the third degree before the final decision would be made as to whether or not they would let them go with me.

The first letter I received from them after the Muskegon trip, both girls stated, "Coach, you passed the inspection with flying colors." Praise God how quickly Christians can become friends and have faith in each other.

Up In The Air

GOD GOES TO SCHOOL / 143

A Christian teacher in a public high school, somehow, was granted permission to have me speak in his five classes about the Bible. He also arranged for me to speak to the newly organized Bible Club for the first meeting on released time. Some Christian students had placed many posters in the halls inviting students to come to the first Bible Club meeting to hear me speak. On the posters, they had described much of my background concerning state championships, and winning teams in football and basketball.

Over one hundred students came to the Bible Club meeting, including several faculty members and the entire coaching staff.

At this meeting, I was able to present God's Plan of Salvation, and just what each one of us had to do to join the Family of God. During the five classes, I talked to the students on the subject of why I knew the Bible is true and accurate, and how it can solve our problems. This seemed logical enough to tell, and logical to discuss why I knew the world's best seller is true. I was able to make friends with the students and answered many questions.

I also chatted with many students in the hallways. I was invited into three staggered lunch hour periods where I told the students about the Bible as they ate their lunch. During the day, I casually mentioned that I was going out to the airport after school, and I would have a little time to take some of them up in my plane and over the city if they desired to come out. I ended up taking sixteen plane loads, and over sixty students for a ride in my plane.

That night we had a gym party and a swimming party, and invited all interested students to attend a meeting at a certain church after the parties. One hundred teenagers came to the meeting and many were saved and strengthened in their faith. It was after midnight when I spoke to the last teenager waiting to see me. Praise God, because He has such a compassion for teenagers.

Three weeks later, I called the Christian teacher, "Pete, I want to know what whiplash you received from the administration, faculty, parents, and teenagers. It will help me in future contacts."

"Floyd," Pete answered, "I asked for complaints from all groups and did not receive any from anyone."

Pete went on to tell me that all remarks were appreciative and good. I believe that we are running scared. If the approach is right and proper, students, administrators and faculty are willing and even eager to have the Bible presented.

A Winning Mistake

Williamston High School was playing for the state basketball championship back in 1940 against Keego Harbor in Jenison Field House at Michigan State in East Lansing, Michigan. I was fortunate to be the Williamston basketball coach at the time. Keego Harbor had won 57 out of 59 games over a three year period, and had an excellent team. However, with some new innovations in basketball, such as the zone full court press, fast break and race horse basketball, and the one-handed jump shot, we had worked our way into the finals.

At half-time against Keego Harbor, we had a 25 to 11 lead. A fourteen point lead might not sound like much of a lead, but at that time, it was the same as a thirty point lead today. I knew if we continued to play the type of ball we played the first half that we would have our first state championship.

As our players trooped into the locker room for the half-time recess, I saw them staring at those large championship trophies. I knew that I needed to keep their minds off the score and the big lead we had, so I was talking rapidly about improvements needed for the second half.

The locker room door opened, and a photographer rushed in and exclaimed, "Coach, let me take a picture of the next state champions!"

I turned that photographer around and booted him right through that locker room door.

I could tell by the expressions on my player's faces that the damage had been done. I never did see the photographer again, but he must have been from Keego Harbor. As the second half was ending, Keego Harbor came down and made a shot that tied the game at 35 all.

A large round basketball scoreboard was being used in Jenison Field House. For the last minute of play the scoreboard would turn red, and after the last sixty seconds the board would turn white -- and the game would be over. When Keego Harbor tied the game up at 35 all, I looked up at the scoreboard and it was red and indicated 42 seconds left.

My five foot, eight inch guard, Dave, came dribbling down the side of the great mammoth field house court. As he dribbled past me at the center of that large college court, I shouted at him, "Shoot it, Dave, shoot it, Dave."

Just as Dave let go of the ball, I thought: what a stupid coach you are, Eby. Don't you know that Dave is the worst shot in the whole school. We have girls that can shoot better than Dave, and here you are ordering him to take the most important shot of the season.

Dave was a marvelous defensive player, passer, play-maker, and rebounder, but he just couldn't shoot. All year long I had been forbidding him to shoot.

My story would end now, if I could tell you he made that shot from the center of the court and won the game. But he didn't.

Keego Harbor picked off the rebound, dribbled it down the court, and worked it around and then shot it.

Fortunately, they missed the shot, but Keego Harbor snatched their own rebound and passed it back out and started working it around again.

I knew that time had to be out. And I expected the sound of the gun at any moment. Keego Harbor shot once again and missed. Dave jumped up in the air under the defensive board, and snapped that rebound down in his strong hands, and started dribbling down the same path once again -- right past me.

But by this time I had really smartened up, and I yelled, "Shoot it, Dave, shoot it, Dave!"

And Dave once again let it go from the center of the court.

The ball hit the backboard and zipped through the net!

I looked up at that large round scoreboard, and it was still red. As I looked at it, the board turned white, and the game was officially over, and we had won the state championship.

However, it seemed as if I was the only person out of thirteen thousand that knew it. No one could hear the gun at the scorer's table, and the players and officials kept going up and down the court playing the game. I rushed out on the court in my suit and tie, and started chasing the ball. The third time down the court I got the ball, and we were still ahead. We won!

I had been afraid that Keego Harbor would score a three point play and through a misunderstanding at the scorer's table we would lose the state championship. This was the first year that Williamston High School had ever won even a district championship, and this year we went all the way.

Even though our home was only twelve miles from East Lansing, we were staying in a Lansing Hotel, because the state was paying our expenses. The next morning, the team and I climbed out of bed to prepare to go back to Williamston and attend one of our local churches as a team.

I bought a Lansing State Journal.

There on the front page was my picture with large headlines, "Boy coaching wonder wins state championship in first year of coaching."

On the second page was a picture of Governor Dickinson. I thought this was great, but it was some time later when my Lord showed me humility. He indicated to me that I was in coaching not to win and promote Floyd Eby, but to have contacts and opportunities to promote the cause of Christ.

Praise God that He knows how to make a coach humble, by losing games.

Now Is Not The Acceptable Time

After coaching and teaching four years at Williamston High School, I moved to Coldwater High School, Coldwater, Michigan. I was head football coach as well as head basketball coach. When I started coaching the football team I knew very few boys by name as they were all new to me. The second week of football practice, we were scrimmaging, and I was trying to show my halfback, Joe, how to run the left end.

I said to Joe, "There are two ways to do it; first as we snapped the ball to you through the quarterback's legs, you will take your first two steps up toward the tackle hole, and as the defensive end sucks in, the wingback will hit him. Then you will pivot on your right foot and cut off the tail of the wingback and head for the sidelines and daylight; you understand, Joe?"

"Yeh, Coach," Joe confirmed.

I continued, "Now, Joe, the other way is to take your first two steps parallel to the line of scrimmage. The defensive end will start to cover you wide, our left guard will pull and block him out. You will pivot up field on your left foot, cut off the tail of our blocking guard, and when through the hole, head for the sidelines and daylight."

"Yeh, Coach," Joe agreed.

However, Joe could not seem to get the right technique, so I told him to watch me.

Being the coach, I did not have on a football uniform; just football cleats, baseball pants, whistle, and T shirt. Huddling up, I called my play number, and received the ball. I took the first two steps up toward the tackle hole, the defensive end sucked in, our wingback hit him from the outside. I pivoted on my right foot, and cut off the tail of our wingback and headed for the sidelines and daylight.

I was speeding along carrying the pigskin for about thirty yards, when something hit me right at the knees like a ton of bricks.

As I was going down, I thought to myself, I want to know that boy's name; anyone who can hit like that, I can use.

As I settled to the ground with this guy on top of me, I could hardly wait to learn his name. A 195 pounder got off me, and I jumped to my feet and said, "What is your name, son?"

He answered, "Carl."

I was thinking, I hope Carl is only a junior and not a senior, so I can use him for two years. I said, "What grade are you in, Carl?"

"Sixth," he answered.

Here Carl was a sixth grader down practicing with the varsity. I had to wait patiently three years before I could use him four straight years as my varsity fullback.

By then he had grown up, still five feet, eight inches tall, but now 245 pounds, and he was incredibly hard to bring down. I praise God for Carl because he not only became my fullback, but also became my brother in Christ. He and his wife also have two fine Christian athletes of their own.

Just Talking

Starting basketball practice on one Monday night near the end of the season, I was having an instructional session with my varsity players. I was explaining to them about Marshall, this Friday's opposition.

"Fellows, as you know, Marshall has only won one game all year, and we have not lost a game yet. I warn you that Marshall is a lot better than their record shows, and they have nothing to lose, and everything to gain. Frankly, we cannot afford a loss at this stage of the season before the tournaments. If we become over confident, conceited, and don't work hard this week, we could lose this game."

I preached this to them again on Tuesday, Wednesday and Thursday, and on Friday, we played Marshall High School and lost.

A coach soon loses his popularity when he loses a ball game -- especially one he was supposed to win. Like the coach who, after losing a ball game, walked out into the gym lobby and asked a man to loan him a dime to call a friend. The man gave him twenty cents and told him to call all his friends. The coach found out that he had to give one dime back, because the only friend he had left was his wife.

To make this Marshall loss worse, it was a home game. As I was walking the three blocks home, wondering whether I should pray to the Lord or hang myself from the garage rafters, I looked up at the stars, and said to myself, "Eby, where did you fail?"

Then I had to honestly ask myself, had I really believed that lousy, scrubby, terrible team from Marshall could beat us? I had to honestly answer, no. You see, friends, all week long as I preached to my team, I really didn't believe what I was saying. In fact, I was "just talking," and therefore I did not communicate to my players. They didn't know, and I didn't know that I didn't really believe what I was telling them. But because I didn't really believe, I wasn't able to convince my players of the need and therefore we lost.

I believe today, spiritually, that many of us are "just talking" church, witnessing, Bible, prayer, Christian service, and therefore we are not communicating this wonderful news to others.

Let us quit "just talking" and communicate Jesus to others who need Him!

The Truth Shall Set You Free

We read in John 8:32, *And ye shall know the truth, and the truth shall make you free.*

As an athletic coach and athletic director, I was very stringent on training rules. The boys were able to help set up the rules for their team, but once the rules were established, they either obeyed them, or were removed from the team. I never considered myself kicking a player off the team, but the player himself removed himself from the team as soon as he broke the rules.

My psychology of questioning was such that a boy would always admit his guilt when I was talking to him alone. As I would question him, I could see the anxiety, strain, stress, and fear while trying to get around the actual truth.

Eventually, as he broke down and admitted his guilt, even though he knew by his admittance, he was going to lose what he loved the most, playing on the team, I could see a real look of relief going over his countenance, as the truth came out. No longer did he have to live the lie when he came face to face with me each time. No longer did he have to worry about some one reporting him. No longer did he have to continually cover up his wrongdoing, but as it states in John 8:32, *And ye shall know the truth, and the truth shall make you free.* Praise God that His Word is always right!

*Lay not up for yourselves treasures upon earth,
where moth and rust doth corrupt, and where thieves
break through and steal. But lay up for yourselves
treasures in Heaven, where neither moth nor rust
doth corrupt, and where thieves do not break through
nor steal. For where your treasure is, there
will your heart be also.*
Matthew 6:19-21

11

GOD IS IN BUSINESS

Raise The Price

It was necessary for me to repossess a house and lot in
Sturgis, Michigan. The people to whom I had sold the
property had not made any payments for a couple of years;
they had moved out and abandoned it, leaving it in a mess. I
wrote them a check for their equity and had them sign a quit
claim deed. They were happy to sign the deed, because they
had not expected to receive any money.

My investment was approximately ten thousand dollars
which was about market value appraisal. However, it was in a
commercial zone. I covenanted with the Lord that any profit
coming from this "repo" would go one hundred per cent to
His Missionary Work.

A man offered me twelve thousand, but the deal didn't work.

I meditated with God. "Lord," I asked, "Why didn't that deal go through? Don't you want the money, or isn't the price high enough?"

I raised my price to fifteen thousand, and a man came along and offered that much, and I accepted. However, eventually the man backed out and the deal was gone.

I raised the price to eighteen thousand, and a man came along and put two hundred and fifty dollars down toward this price. The state gave him some difficulty on driveways coming off of Highway M-66 to the property, so he forfeited his deposit and backed out of the deal.

By this time I was somewhat discouraged.

"Lord," I asked, "Don't you want the money? Is it too much or not enough?"

I raised the price to twenty thousand dollars, and a client signed an agreement to pay that much, but once again it fell through. However, I was still stubborn and believed God could use the money, and I raised the price to twenty-two thousand.

Once again a customer offered that much, but again the deal fell through.

"Lord, the only thing I know to do is to keep raising the price,"

This time the price went to twenty-five thousand dollars, and recently I closed a solid deal at that price.

I have no regrets, because I know this is the amount that the Lord wanted, or else it would not have gone through. Praise God that we can come to him in faith concerning business dealings, if we will commit them to Him completely.

It Doesn't Pay the Bills

A new local filling station opened up in town, and I started doing all my business at this one station. A young lady by the name of Sherry operated and managed the station. I made friends with her, and had something special to say to her each time I drove in. She treated me well, but she and her employees seemed to think of me as "that Jesus man."

At the station I was continually telling her that God and the Bible had all the answers to all of her problems.

She kept answering me, "But the Bible and God don't pay the bills."

However, Sherry continued to show more interest, and one evening she came to my house to see me. We went down into my recreation room in the basement, and I opened the scriptures and told Sherry about God's Wonderful Plan for her life. She accepted the Lord that evening and joined the Family of God. Sherry has told me several times she is reading the Bible and praying, and how God has helped her in so many ways. Sherry has found out that God can and will supply her needs as she commits her life to Him!

Let God Make The Decisions

I am vice president of a cablevision corporation. Although I have been a businessman for many years, I know very little about electronics. The president of our corporation is a very intelligent man, and is an expert in electronics. I am perfectly satisfied to sit back and let our president make the decisions on the necessary technical matters of the corporation. He knows what he is doing, and his decisions make me money.

Due to my lack of knowledge, my decisions on these same matters could lead the company into bankruptcy. I think of this many times during necessary spiritual decisions.

Spiritually, we have the greatest president, the greatest chairman of the board, and the greatest executive ever, the Lord Jesus Christ!

Doesn't it make sense to let Jesus make our decisions?

If we try to make the decisions, certainly it will lead to spiritual bankruptcy. God never makes a mistake. If a mistake is made, then it is our decision, not God's!

God And One Is A Majority

When I was selling real estate as a sideline to my teaching and coaching, I had a deal underway that would bring me in my largest commission ever. The deal consisted of a sales agreement on a piece of high priced commercial property. My commission was to be in excess of four thousand dollars. Although I had the necessary signatures of both the sellers and the purchasers on an agreed price, bottlenecks were present. Ultimately, the sellers decided not to sell; the buyers decided not to buy, and I was the only interested party who wanted the deal to go through. Because the signed sales contract was a legal contract, several lawyers, on each side, were involved in the attempt to nullify the sale. I had planned on this four thousand dollars, and had worked on this sale for nearly two years. I finally gave up, and told the Lord, "No way is this deal going through, Lord. However, if you want the total commission, you put the deal through, and the four thousand dollars is yours. Within two months, the transaction was completely closed, and the Lord had the four thousand dollars in His Missionary Work. I praise Him that He is an able God, and with Him all things are possible!

God Can Use It

Part of one of my residential subdivisions was some swamp land near a river. Citizens in the area had a project underway to clean up the chain of lakes and the river and had assessed the swamp land. In order to eliminate the assessments on some worthless land, I decided to give it away. However, no one wanted it, would not accept it, so I was forced to keep it.

I told the Lord that if He sold the land, He would receive one hundred per cent of it to purchase and distribute Bibles.

Soon after, a man approached me and wanted to know if he could purchase that small piece of swamp land between his lot and the river. I charged him five hundred dollars, and thanked the Lord as he paid me.

The next day, the man's neighbor came to see me and he purchased the chunk of land between his lot and the river for five hundred dollars.

Two weeks later, one of his neighbors also wanted some swamp land in addition to a small pond, and I sold both to him for twenty-five hundred dollars.

Within a month, another man wanted a large parcel of the swamp land between his lot and the river, which he purchased for three thousand dollars.

I could not give the swamp land away, but our Lord took it and used it to purchase and distribute sixty-five hundred dollars of scriptures throughout the world.

Praise God, and He has three more parcels of swamp land that He can sell at His accepted time!

He Leased Quarters In Heaven For Free

I rented some farm land to a farmer and his wife. One day they came to my office to make the final payment. I did not know anything about their spiritual status. As they started to leave my foyer, I started to talk to them about my faith in God. The couple stood there and listened for about twenty minutes, and then left. I didn't see them again for several months until I was serving as a pall bearer at my neighbor's funeral who was a relative of this farmer called Gary.

At the cemetery, Gary got out of his car and came over to me and shook my hand. He said, "Floyd, I want you to know that I appreciated that talk we had in your home several months ago. It has been of help to me."

"I'm glad to hear that, Gary," I replied as we parted.

Upon arriving home, I told my wife that I believed Gary wanted to talk to me. I called him. "Gary, I really appreciated your comments at the cemetery, but I have a feeling you would like to talk with me some more."

"That's right," he exclaimed. "I would like to have you come out and talk with me, my wife, and daughter."

As we tried to set up a time, we determined that it would have to be at night, because his wife worked all day, and his daughter was in school. However, I didn't have a night free for three weeks so I suggested, "Gary, what about me coming out and talking with you at ten o'clock tomorrow morning? We can talk with the rest of your family later."

He agreed. I believe, if we feel the Lord is leading, we

should not postpone an encounter.

The next morning, I drove out to see Gary, and he told me, "Ever since you talked to me that day in your home, I have been reading the Bible. But there are many things I don't understand." I found out later that Gary had been excommunicated from a church, and had developed a real hatred toward all religion.

I opened the scriptures, and told Gary about God's wonderful plan for his life. I also explained how he could have this new way of life, by just taking the needed steps to join the Family of God according to the Bible. Gary accepted God's Gift of Eternal Life.

"I want you to be sure and come out to talk with my wife and daughter," Gary commented. "You know my wife is going to think I am crazy, but I don't care, because I really believe."

Several weeks later, I met with Gary, his wife, Jean and their daughter, Doris. The family had lost a boy two years earlier in a hunting accident. I presented Jean and Doris with two Bibles each, and presented God's Plan. I praise God that the entire family are now my brother and sisters in Christ. What a beautiful family, and how I love them.

Don't Squeeze The Last Nickel

I was taking bids on the construction of roads in one of my subdivisions. I invited the bidding road contractors to meet with the county road engineer and me at the site at a certain time.

As we walked the subdivision with the topography charts and specifications, I carefully explained that I was going to accept the low bid and give that amount of money to the road commission. The commission would pay them as they satisfactorily completed the job.

I emphasized that the bid must include a satisfactory performance that the commission would approve. One of my former students and athletes, Terry, quoted the low bid, and got the job.

As a businessman, I drove for a hard, honest bargain, and always held the low bidder responsible to stand by his bid and agreed responsibilities.

Some time after the road construction was started, Terry came to me, "Coach," he said, "When I bid off this job, I assumed that under the top soil, the gravel would be good enough to be used as an approved base for the processed gravel. The road commission won't O.K. it, and I will have to haul gravel in for the proper base. It's throwing my bid way off."

I was just ready to answer Terry that he was properly warned, and it was his mistake, and he would have to stand the loss. However, I believe that I had a leading from God, because Floyd Eby would not have said, "Go ahead, Terry, and haul the base gravel in, and I will pay you the extra money it costs you."

Terry was pleasantly surprised, because he knew my reputation for sticking to contracts and driving hard bargains.

Several weeks later, I saw Terry walk down the aisle of our church accepting Jesus as Saviour. I shudder when I think I might not have felt God's leading, and had insisted on sticking with our original agreement. I might have been a stumbling block to Terry's salvation. I was supposed to have represented Christ as a professing Christian. I praise God for His many leadings over the years that have taken me to needy people in time; leadings which have also prevented me from losing my testimony.

God Is A Tax Expert

The Internal Revenue Service sent me a letter stating they had audited three years of my federal tax returns and had found some mistakes.

I owed IRS an additional fifteen thousand dollars in tax, and was to remit within ten days.

I immediately called them and set up an appointment. The disagreement was over the sale of subdivision lots. My certified public accountant had taken long term capital gains on the sale of the lots, which meant paying on only half of the profit. IRS didn't believe these lots qualified for such treatment. The IRS indicated that they knew I had not done anything purposefully wrong; that it was strictly a matter of a difference of opinion. It was definitely a marginal, gray area of decision, and the courts were jammed with similar cases. However, IRS continued to disagree on the handling of the sales of these lots. I continued to appeal it until I was sent to Detroit.

I did not take my lawyer or C.P.A., but after much prayer I decided to go only by myself and God.

As I presented my case, I tried in the love of Christ, to indicate my Christianity and my love and concern for my country. I also pointed out that if I could be shown where I was definitely wrong, I would borrow the money and pay the government.

The IRS agent was very polite and respectful, and seemed to be pleased that I alone came to present my case. He had to deal mostly with lawyers, and C.P.A.'s in cases involving this much money.

After much studying and discussion, we arrived at a procedure which lowered the tax owed to eight thousand dollars. I asked him what chance I would have if I went to court, and he said only a 30-70 chance of winning. I settled and praise God for His goodness.

Recently, I received a letter from the State of Michigan concerning a three year audit on my state income tax. They wanted seven thousand dollars additional tax. At this time I was retired, and my income was low compared to my church and charitable contributions. With all my exemptions, my taxable income was a thousand dollars per year or less.

However, I had this problem with the state: For many years I had land contract payments coming in on homes which I had mortgaged at the bank. The contract payment would go directly to the bank and be applied on my mortgage. I would take in approximately fifty thousand dollars in interest each year, and pay out to the bank approximately forty-nine thousand dollars in interest. My CPA would declare one thousand dollars net interest as income.

A few years later the IRS made me declare all fifty thousand dollars of interest as adjusted gross income, and then allowed me to deduct the forty-nine thousand dollars of interest paid out as a deductible expense. This was fine, as it came out with the same results.

However, the State of Michigan calculated my state income tax from the amount of adjusted gross income on my Federal tax return. The state would not allow any deductions including my forty-nine thousand dollars interest expense. This meant each year I was paying state tax on forty-nine thousand dollars that I never made or received.

As I arrived at my appointed hearing, I received condolences and sympathy, but they said there was nothing they could do about it because it was the law. They would turn it over to their staff of attorneys, and see what could be done.

I told them to tell the lawyers that they needed to come up with something, because this was unfair, and I could not pay a tax on money I never made.

The lawyers came back with the original amount plus some extra penalities. I appealed for another hearing, and these men really seemed to be concerned about my problem. They felt it unfair, but finally came to the conclusion that their hands were tied because no way could they change or circumvent the law. They informed me that nothing could be done.

I went home sad, but upon arriving, I took it to the greatest tax expert of all, Jesus Christ. I went to my knees and asked Him for help, and also a leading.

After much prayer, I felt led to rearrange my state tax return to include paying state tax on interest paid on general notes, but not on interest paid on mortgages. I presented my case prayerfully by letter with the love of Christ in my heart.

I mailed the state a check for eighteen hundred dollars instead of seven thousand dollars, and prayed that God would see that this would suffice in spite of the unfair law.

Months later, praise God, I received a letter and a receipt accepting this settlement.

Once again, the money went to God's Work. I praise Him that I can bring all things to a God who loves me and is concerned about me.

But ye shall receive power, after that the
Holy Ghost is come upon you; and ye shall
be witnesses unto me both in Jerusalem, and in all
Judea, and in Samaria, and unto the
uttermost part of the earth.
Acts 1:8

12

TELLING OTHERS

God Will Use You If You Are Available

I personally do not like to use any terminology about witnessing that would indicate that Floyd Eby had anything to do with a person entering the Kingdom of God.

I clearly understand that only the Holy Spirit of God, and the individual's own decision to accept this gift of God in faith can bring about this miracle of joining the Family of God. I do realize that as Christians refer to Soul Winners, winning a person to Christ, leading a person to Christ, personal witnessing, etc., they do not mean to take any credit, but I sometimes feel that other people misinterpret the terminology.

Therefore, I like to use the term of "Being used of God, as a servant of God."

I believe our Lord will use each one of us in a special way if we make ourselves available to be used. God will do all the rest, and He is the only one who can do the rest. Also God will use each one of us differently as to the abilities that He has endowed us with, and He does not expect us to be used the same way as others are used.

Acts 1:8 *But ye shall receive power, after that the Holy Ghost is come upon you; and ye shall be witnesses unto me both in Jerusalem, and in all Judaea, and in Samaria, and unto the uttermost part of the earth.*

You notice, friends, God has given all Christians a command to go and tell the Good News. He told us to go to all around us, and then expand to a larger area, and then to all parts of the world.

Many times people say they cannot understand the Bible, but God only holds us responsible for that part of His Word that we do understand, or in other words, that part which He has already revealed to us. I am sure all of us can understand, *Ye shall be witnesses unto me.*

One day I realized that the word *shall* in the English language is a command, and I understood it. I cannot tell Jesus when I face Him that I didn't understand it, because I do. It is not easy to be used of God as a servant of God, but if we are close to God, He will use each one of us in His accepted way. God gave us all different talents and abilities, and will use us accordingly. Some may be used by just the way they live their lives pleasing to God. Others by special talent such as singing, instrumental music, speaking, making friends, helping others, teaching, athletics, etc. Different personalities are used differently with different people. In certain situations, and with certain individuals, God will use different specific individuals to be used of God. The only real importance is our willingness to be used.

I would like to quote two verses of scripture which have meant so much to my life in being used of God as a servant of God. 1 Corinthians 9:19 *For though I be free from all men, yet have I made myself servant unto all, that I might gain the more.* Ephesians 6:19 *And for me, that utterance may be given unto me, that I may open my mouth boldly, to make known the mystery of the gospel.*

These two verses of scripture mean that Floyd Eby should

be willing to sacrifice any and all things to be available to be used of God. I must be willing to allow God to set my priorities, and schedule my time if I am going to be really available to be used of Him.

I believe no one can be used of God with an individual unless that individual accepts you as a friend, loves you, respects you, or has confidence in you. So many times I have to spend much time making friends with people before I ever mention Jesus to them. It may take several visits, or only a few minutes depending on the individual.

We also need to recognize the difference between resentment and resistance. All unbelievers will have some resistance to hearing about Jesus, or they would already have become believers. Therefore, if they show friendly resistance, perhaps God has prepared them, and we should continue to be used of God with them. However, if the individual resents you talking to them about Jesus, you should immediately stop. God has not yet prepared them and you are wasting your time and their time, and are also setting up a greater barrier for the future. If they don't believe that there is a God, I find it is no use talking to them about Christianity. Just pray that God will reveal Himself to them and open the door in the future.

As you are talking to people about Jesus, always give them an opportunity to "turn you off" if they so desire. An effective way I have is to say, "If you don't like what I am saying, all you have to do is tell me to 'turn off, Coach,' and we will talk about sports, weather, flying, keep quiet, or I will just leave."

This statement puts the unbeliever in control, and he will hardly ever tell you to stop, because he knows he can if he so desires. It also makes the individual reluctant to admit to you that he is afraid to hear about this new way of life.

When I first meet a person and become his or her friend, and I believe that God has opened the door for me to speak to him about Jesus, I give him a new testament presented as a gift from Floyd Eby with my address and telephone number in it. I also print his name in it. It is difficult for a person to throw a gift away that has been presented to him with his name in it. After I am through talking with him, I always tell him that if he has a spiritual problem -- and all problems are spiritual -- just write to me or call me collect. As God opens the door, I visit him and go over the scriptures with my new friend. After I give him the new testament, I first tell him how, at one time, I didn't believe the Bible, but I now know it is true, and I know it is the answer to all of my problems. I tell him why I am convinced that it is true, and then I go through the presentation of God's Plan for his life as presented in Chapter three.

If a person rejects Jesus, I don't let it upset me one bit. I just say, "You know that is the wonderful thing about our Jesus, He doesn't force Himself on anyone. He gives everyone a free choice, and no one has to go to Heaven if he doesn't want to. Isn't that wonderful? I am still your friend and I will continue to pray that Jesus will reveal Himself to you."

If the person professes Jesus Christ as his or her personal Saviour, and joins the Family of God, I then tell him the importance of becoming a close friend of Jesus, as told in Chapter Four.

I recognize that "open doors" and opportunities supplied by our Saviour are very important in being used of God as a servant of God. But I do not believe in grabbing someone by the collar, and demanding an answer to the question, "Are you saved?" I believe such drastic steps are not necessary, and are not efficient. I sincerely believe that as we become available to be used of God, that our Lord will open many doors to people with hearts already prepared by Him. It will be readily apparent that this door was opened for us.

If we are truly available, God will give us more opportunities than we can handle. We will never have to force a door open. Most of the rest of this book will tell how the author has been involved in walking through "open doors" prepared by Jesus; through no doors prepared by Floyd Eby. We should be just as happy when a person rejects Jesus as when he accepts Him. We have been used of God, and we can do no more. The rest is up to the individual and the Holy Spirit. We have been willing and available to be used of God as a servant of God, and that is what is really important.

Praise God for all of the opportunities.

Do It God's Way

Since I have had so many opportunities to present seminars on being used of God to many Christian people, I have found a problem in using a fellow Christian in the demonstration. The Christian does not react like an unbeliever. In fact, he presents many problems that an unbeliever doesn't.

The Christian, in a sense, attempts to give you somewhat of a bad time, and asks questions that unbelievers wouldn't, and the response is actually artificial. Because of these experiences in training seminars, I have had the urge to go out on the street, and select an unbeliever whom I don't know, pay him for his time, and tell him I wanted to use him in a training demonstration. Then I would have the real thing before my Christian observers, and it would make no difference whether the person accepted or rejected Jesus.

For two years, I tried to work up courage to do it this way, and each time just before the training session, I would "chicken" out. I would end up calling on some Christian to help me, and once again I would have the artificial situation.

Finally, I was holding such a meeting in the Holiday Inn in Traverse City, Michigan, and I arrived early to prepare the facilities. I started to talk to a young man on the hotel staff. He told me his father was a doctor, but he was dying of cancer, and this young man was also taking up medicine. From his conversation, I deducted that he wasn't a believer. I thought to myself, this is the right time to use an unbeliever in my training seminar. All I will have to do is go to the hotel management, offer to pay for an hour of his wages, and then use him in my presentation.

There was no doubt in my mind that this was the time, and I was definitely going through with it. Then the Lord spoke to me. (I don't hear voices, but I *feel* what He is saying to me.) "Eby, you know better than that. You know only the Holy Spirit brings people into the Kingdom of God. You also know if you bring a stranger in front of a training session as an exhibition, it will quench my Holy Spirit, and leave it up to you, and that just won't work."

Right then, I thanked the Lord for showing me I was wrong. I asked Him why He didn't tell me two years ago so I would not have spent so much time thinking and wondering about trying this experiment. Then I realized that God knew each time that I was going to "chicken out." So He told me nothing. When He knew I was going to "foul" up the works, He let me know in no uncertain terms that it was a crazy idea and would not work, and it would displease Him!

That evening during the meal, three strangers walked in, twin brothers and a girl friend. I immediately went back to greet them as they sat at the banquet table. I introduced myself, and found that the twin brothers were named Jed and Ted. At previous training seminars, I always selected Christians who I personally knew.

This night as I started making my presentation, I said, "Ted, would you like to take part in this presentation?"

I couldn't really believe that I had invited a Christian guest to take part. Ted, without any hesitation, said he would be glad to and immediately came to the speaker's table.

As I proceeded through the presentation with Ted, the response was excellent with no problems. Afterwards, I thanked Ted and told him that he could now go back to his seat.

When the meeting was over, Ted came to me. "You know when you said you were going to choose someone to take part, I was praying that you would ask my twin brother, Jed, because he isn't saved. When you asked me instead, I knew it was God's Will. I realize that if you had asked Jed, he would have been embarrassed before a strange gathering, and he would have rebelled. But by choosing me, so Jed could hear his twin brother go through God's Plan, I am sure it has touched his heart." A few minutes later, Jed came and spoke to me. "Mr. Eby, I have never heard God's Plan presented like that before. It got to me. Sometime in the future, I would like to talk with you more about it."

I then made a second mistake. Jed and I had made some

general plans to get together the next time I flew to Traverse City. He was to have written to me proposing some dates and more details. But he didn't write. I had felt I was too busy that night with my many responsibilities to take time off to talk with Jed. I had to fly all the way back to Coldwater and the weather was threatening. But I should have discarded all these "reasons" and set my priorities straight. When God has prepared a heart, we should be available.

I flew home that night knowing I had made a mistake. I had missed a real opportunity presented to me by our Lord.

Several months passed before I had another opportunity to meet Jed. Then one day I flew into the Traverse City airport, and I called his home number.

His wife answered, and told me Jed was still at work, but she gave me his office telephone number. I called him at his office, and he seemed happy to hear from me.

"Jed, I have a meeting tonight at the Holiday Inn," I said. "What about coming over to your house after the meeting about ten o'clock? You know we agreed that first night I met you that we wanted to meet again and discuss the Bible." He remembered our first meeting and invited me to his home.

My companion and I arrived at Jed's home and received a cordial greeting. After a few minutes of general conversation, I started through God's Plan of Salvation. Just when Jed seemed to become interested, his wife, Ann, came in and Jed introduced her. Ann sat down and started listening. After a few minutes she sarcastically asked, "Do you think all of this will help you with your business?"

I thought to myself, "Oh no, Lord, did you have to send a skeptic in at this time to foul things up?" But aloud I said, "It sure will, Ann." I proceeded to tell her about some business deals that the Lord had brought about.

Ann asked a couple of more skeptical questions, but then started listening intently. She professed Jesus that night, and joined the Family of God. But Jed would not take the necessary step of faith. He said, "I know I need to, I understand it, but I just cannot accept these steps by faith."

Jed asked me where I was going to spend the night. I told

him that I was unable to fly back to Coldwater because of the bad weather. I was going to have Phil drop me off at a motel, and I would fly home the next day.

Ann and Jed asked me to stay at their house overnight, but I told them I wouldn't consider it. I had not known them long enough and didn't want to inconvenience them. I insisted I would stay at a motel. However, Ann and Jed insisted that I should stay with them. I finally consented, as I thought it might be the Lord's Will. I felt good about their sincere invitation, because it meant that Jed and Ann had truly accepted me as their friend.

The next morning I met their three children. I fell in love with this entire beautiful family. Jed drove me to the airport on his way to work. I have corresponded and called this family several times, and Jed drove to Cadillac, Michigan to hear me speak about Jesus. I feel confident that Jed is now a child of God.

During this experience God taught me to walk through the door as soon as He opens it!

I Believe You Have A Point There, Mister

Whenever the weather is too bad for flying, and I have to drive my car, I look for hitchhikers. If I see one, and the Lord leads me to pick him up, I do so and then talk to him about Jesus.

I was driving home on the freeway from Gaylord, Michigan around two o'clock in the morning. I passed a young girl and boy of about twenty years of age, hitchhiking. It was beginning to rain. I stopped, and seeing no traffic behind me, backed up and offered the couple a ride. They both got in the front seat, the girl next to me. I pulled back on the freeway, and kicked it up to seventy miles an hour, which then was the speed limit. The rain intensified, and became a real cloudburst. I handed each of them a Bible as I started to talk to them about the Bible and Jesus.

The girl said, "Listen, Mister, I don't believe in that Bible, God and Jesus you are talking about. I think it is all nonsense."

Perhaps you would rather I wouldn't talk about it," I replied. "All you have to say is, turn it off, Coach, and we will talk about sports, weather, or just keep quiet."

"You can talk about it all you want to. I could care less," she countered. "I just want to get you straightened out in the beginning. I don't believe in it -- and never will. But go ahead and talk all you want."

"Are you ever going to die?" I asked her.

She answered, "No." That reply threw a wrench into my plan of presentation.

Then I asked her, "Don't you see people around you dying every day?"

"Yes," but informed me that she, herself, would not die.

I said, "Lady, I have news for you; do you see that it is raining so hard I cannot see anything in front of this car? If you notice the speedometer, it reads seventy miles per hour. I regret to inform you that you are now riding with the world's worst driver, and you are right next to death."

She replied, "Mister, I have been watching your driving, and I believe you have a point there."

Thereafter, she listened as I told her about the Bible and Jesus all the way to Lansing, Michigan, where I left her and the young man. She did not make a profession, but as she got out of the car, she held up the testament I had given her, "Mister," she said, "I am going to take this Bible home and read it all the way through."

Praise God, the rest is up to her and the Holy Spirit.

It Is Your Fault, Lord

Because of bad weather, I was driving home from Detroit on the I-94 Freeway. As I passed a couple of trucks, I noticed a young man on the berm of the road, hitchhiking with a sign marked, "Albion." I surmised that he was hitchhiking back to Albion College.

As I always do now, I felt bad because I had missed another "open door" the Lord had presented to me. I thought, I would have had fifty miles to talk to that young man about Jesus. "You blew it, Eby," I muttered. I was really raking myself over when I suddenly thought, "You know it wasn't my fault, Lord, I was passing two trucks on the freeway, and there was no way that I could reach that young man by turning around on this freeway. You know, Lord, it was your fault, not mine. If you wanted me to pick up that young man you should have had me in the right lane, not the passing lane."

After throwing the blame on God, I felt better and forgot it. Twenty miles down the road, I saw the same hitchhiker. Someone had picked him up and buzzed him around me and let him off at the side of the road again.

I was now in the right lane, and I remarked, "I got the message, Lord." I pressed hard on the brakes, and came to a screeching halt. I opened the door and said, "Get in, friend. Here is a copy of the Bible, and I want to tell you about Jesus." He took the Bible and got in, and before we reached Albion College, he had professed Christ, and had joined the Family of God.

As I was relating this incident to one of my friends, he remarked, "The trouble with you, Eby, is that you don't have enough faith."

I asked him what he meant.

"The Lord was proving to you that you only needed thirty miles instead of fifty miles to tell this young man about Jesus."

Praise God that He can eliminate our excuses, when He wants an individual to enter His Kingdom!

Be Careful, Susan. This Man Is Going To Try And Get Us Saved

As part of the youth program of a Christian conference in Petoskey, Michigan I was giving youngsters free airplane rides out of the Harbor Springs airport, and across the bay to Petoskey. At noon, the bus picked me up to take me back to Petoskey for lunch. On the bus, the director of the nursery introduced me to four girls who had donated their time to supervise the nursery.

I remarked to these four teenagers that they all ought to be given time off to come out and receive their free airplane ride. They were overjoyed with the invitation, and said their parents would bring them out.

That afternoon, the parents, Toby and Susan, not only brought the girls out, but stayed and helped supervise the other children and load and unload the plane each trip.

When I finished I asked Toby and Susan if they would like to fly with me and also take their small child up. They readily agreed.

As we left the ground, Susan became frightened. She grabbed Toby's shoulder ahead of her and asked him if everything was going to be all right. Toby assured her that everything was O.K., but I noticed that he had his fingers crossed as he told her.

When we landed, I told the bus driver to return the bus to Petoskey. I asked Toby and his family to wait until I refueled, then I asked them to drive me to the nearby Holiday Inn.

I was able to get better acquainted with the family as I fueled my plane and rode with them back to Petoskey. Toby dropped me at the Holiday Inn, and I cleaned up and went down to the evening banquet. I remarked to the director of the nursery, "What a nice Christian family Toby, Susan, and the girls are."

She informed me that the girls were Christians but the parents weren't.

"You have to be kidding," I exclaimed.

She assured me that every time Jesus was presented to them, they would reject Him.

I asked her if she would loan her car to me. I drove the car over to Toby's home, and the family had just driven in the driveway from the grocery store.

I jumped out and greeted them. I told them I had fallen in love with their entire family and wanted a few minutes to talk with them.

Immediately, Toby spoke to his wife, "Be careful, Susan, this man is going to try and get us saved."

His statement hit me right square between the eyes and almost stunned me, but I recovered quickly.

"Not so, Toby, I just want to tell you what happened to Floyd Eby."

They were very wholesome about the matter and invited me into the house. We sat down, including the ninth grade daughter, Tammy, and I started telling how Floyd Eby joined the Family of God.

Tammy kept nodding her agreement on everything I said, but the parents could not accept the fact that Jesus would and did die for our sins. "Coach," Susan said, "We appreciate your work and your approach, and your interest in our Family. We know what you are telling us is good, and that Toby and I need it, but we just cannot take that necessary step of faith."

I thanked them for their hospitality. They asked me to come back any time, and I left, returning to the banquet.

The next week, I called and Toby answered the phone. Toby and Susan still had not accepted the Lord, but Toby did say, "You know I was at Traverse City this week and I ran into a friend who was having all kinds of problems, and I told him that what he needed was Jesus." Toby also told me on the phone that while he was in Traverse City, he met a guy that started telling him about Jesus. Toby told him that he had already received that "pitch" from a guy from Coldwater by the name of Floyd Eby.

This "guy" that was now talking to Toby happened to be a personal Christian friend of mine. Toby and Susan are wholesome, friendly, and willing to listen. I have visited and corresponded with them several times, and many of us are praying for them, but to my knowledge, they still have not joined the Family of God.

Praise God that they do not resent their children knowing Jesus. Perhaps, the accepted time has not yet arrived for Toby and Susan. I pray to God that they have not rejected the accepted time.

Putting On A Front

I was making some calls in a mobile home park, and I noticed a young lady out in a yard. I went up to her and shook her hand and said, "I am Coach Eby, what is you name?" She told me Marilyn and I chatted with her a few minutes and then left.

The next week on my rounds, I saw Marilyn again, and shook her hand and made some friendly chatter for a few minutes. I remarked about how cute little Terry and Alice, her children, were, but as yet I had not mentioned Jesus. I was still in the process of making friends and acquiring her trust and confidence.

The following Wednesday, she seemed to be looking for me. I felt the time was right. I asked her if I could come over that night and meet with her and her husband. I want to talk to you about a marvelous new way of life, through the Bible and Jesus.

She said, "Jerry won't like it, but I am going to invite you anyway."

Marilyn called Jerry at his place of work, and informed him that she had met a guy by the name of Coach Eby. This Eby was going to come over and talk with them about the Bible and Jesus. Jerry was unhappy about the arrangements, but he didn't quite know how to get out of it.

As I arrived at the mobile home, Marilyn invited me in. I rushed up to Jerry, shook his hand, and told him how happy I was to be able to meet him. He wasn't impressed. But as I continued to try to win him over as my friend, he lit up a cigarette, and blew smoke in my face.

I paid no attention and continued to chat with him about his job and family. Jerry then went over to the refrigerator, opened a can of beer, and came over close to me and hoisted the beer to his mouth.

Once again, I acted as though I had not noticed. However, within an hour, both Jerry and Marilyn had accepted Jesus, and had joined the Family of God.

Marilyn was the daughter of missionary parents. She had been putting on a front of being a Christian all these years, but had never had a personal encounter with Christ. She called her parents long distance, and told her mother that she had been really saved. Her mother implied that she had heard this before. I told Marilyn to invite her parents for a visit which she did. Marilyn was attending Bible study and church regularly, and was also witnessing to neighbors. She sometimes invited a neighbor in for me to talk to about the Lord, and God used her in several cases. However, Jerry and Marilyn's marriage failed, and she moved to the north where she lacked the Christian fellowship that all Christians desperately need. At times she has been out of fellowship with the Lord, but each time He brings her back. Marilyn has fine Christian parents, but she sometimes rebels at their approach to Christian living.

In spite of the failure of his marriage, Jerry has grown tremendously in the faith, and is being used greatly of God. Jerry is manager of a local eating establishment, and still has a home Bible study in his mobile home every Wednesday night. He also attends a Monday evening Bible study in which he continues to be a strong leader. On Saturday mornings, he attends prayer meeting and breakfast, in spite of the late hours his job demands. He does attend church, but his real witness is outside the church.

He picks up hitchhikers, and talks to them about Jesus, as well as showing real compassion, love and concern for their problems. He has been responsible for inviting many of his employees into the Bible studies. At least a dozen have come to know the Lord through his invitation, including his own brother, Don.

When Jerry hires a new employee, he takes him into his office and tells him that it is necessary to explain about his faith in God. He and many of his employees are Christians, and he wants his new employees to understand what it is all about. In this way the new employee can better understand the manager and his Christian works in order to promote harmony among the workers of his establishment. Jerry has also made several trips with me in my plane to promote the cause of Christ, as well as give his testimony at meetings. Praise God for the young people that are on fire for Jesus.

At Your Own Risk

A couple rented a mobile home from me by mail, before they moved to Coldwater from Florida. I met them at the mobile home. As we visited, the wife said, "We have a thirty year old daughter who came with us, and her life is a mess. She married a bum, had two children, and then became divorced. During this marriage, her three year old daughter was place on a pony by her husband. The pony bolted and ran. The daughter, in falling, was caught by the reins and was dragged to her death. She and her husband had already agreed that he would take the boy and she would have the girl, but now she was left with nothing." The wife continued, "Lou Ann, because of this tragedy, hit the bottle and became involved with drugs. She then married another bum, and has now left him and come back with us."

I asked this woman why she was telling me all this?

She answered, "My husband and I understand that you work with people with problems. Wouldn't you see if you could help Lou Ann?"

I informed the lady that I only work with people if God opens the door, and I use only the spiritual, God and His Holy Word, the Bible. Also I could not help Lou Ann with her problems, but if she would be willing, I could introduce her to Jesus, who could change her life.

Apparently Lou Ann's parents were not believers, but they were desperate, and were willing to try anything with Lou Ann. The mother went on to tell me that Lou Ann wouldn't even stay with them, but had just left the mobile home to live in a motel. She asked me if I would go there to talk with her. I told her I would contact her, but whether I talked to Lou Ann or not would be entirely up to Lou Ann.

I knocked on the motel room door, and Lou Ann opened it.

"Lou Ann, I am Coach Eby," I announced. "I have just been talking with your parents. They asked me to come out to talk with you."

She interrupted, "I am in no mood to have a sermon preached to me."

"Good," I replied, "Because I am in no mood to preach a sermon, so you and I are in the same mood. I just came by to tell you about a new way of life my wife and I have found that is tremendous, as well as being free. However, it is up to you whether I tell you about it or not."

She allowed me to step inside. "Listen, Mister," she said, "You can start talking, but I warn you that you talk at your own risk. You are going to have your feelings hurt, because it will be only a matter of time before I get mad and tell you off, and boot you out of here."

"Wonderful," I exclaimed. "I love people like that, and I will leave any time you tell me to."

Forty-five minutes later, Lou Ann accepted Jesus as Saviour, and joined the Family of God, and became my sister in Christ. We closed our session in prayer, asking God's blessing upon His new child, Lou Ann.

Two nights later, I received a call from a different motel. It was Lou Ann and she wanted me to come over to meet her husband, Mahlon, who had followed her to Michigan. When I arrived at the motel, Lou Ann introduced me to Mahlon. I presented God's Plan of Salvation to Mahlon and he also accepted Christ, and became my brother in Christ. Both of them obtained jobs, started reading the Bible, having family devotions, praying, and attending a home Bible study, and attending church. One time they flew with me on a weekend trip that included two church services and a jail service. Even though they were still having some troubles, their lives were becoming progressively better.

But life became so good that the devil was able to pull them away from all this spiritual fellowship and service.

I refused to "bug" them about it. As I knew would happen, their situation took a turn for the worse, and troubles became abundant again.

I see Mahlon and Lou Ann occasionally, but it is a hit and miss relationship with Jesus. Therefore, God is not blessing them like He would like to, if they would just put Him first in their lives and get to know Him better and better.

I pray for Mahlon and Lou Ann regularly, and I just know

that in time they will see the need of becoming a close friend of Jesus rather than a distant friend.

Praise God that He has patience.

Sowing The Seed

As I was riding a bus in Houston, Texas, I gave a New Testament to the lady bus driver while we were waiting at a stop. I asked her what her name was and wrote it in the Bible along with my name, address and telephone number. I told Lillian that there were four verses underlined in her Bible, and I would like to have her look them up and read them when she had time. She said she would. Several months later, I received a letter from Lillian thanking me for the testament. She told me how Jesus had entered her life, and she was now praising God. I praise God for the power of His Holy Word, and how sown seed will produce fruit.

Taking Nothing For Granted

Bruce, one of my spiritual children with whom I had worked for some time, brought Ruth, his girl friend to church several times, and I just assumed that she was a Christian. One night I received a call from Ruth, wanting me to come see her at her mobile home.

I explained to her that I had Bible studies and appointments until eleven-thirty that night, but would come out after that if she wanted me to. When I arrived, Bruce and Ruth were there. I asked Ruth how I could help her, and Bruce spoke up, "Coach, she used to be married to a Navy man, and she wants to hear some of your Navy stories."

I said it was too late to tell stories, and Ruth interrupted, "I want you to tell me about the Bible and Jesus."

I opened the Bible and took Ruth through the entire plan of salvation, step by step, and she professed Jesus as Saviour, and became my sister in Christ. She went to the phone and called her mother long distance, and said, "Mom, you don't have to worry about me any more. Just now I have really been saved."

God has taught me not to assume or take anything for granted.

Too Close A Friend

The most difficult people for me to witness to are my closest friends and relatives. Many are church goers, but I wonder if they are like Floyd Eby used to be, a church goer without having a personal encounter with Jesus.

One of my closest friends and neighbors, a man for whom I once worked, was one of these persons I was concerned about. But in no way was I going to insult my friend by asking him if he was a Christian.

I put off talking to Aaron and Rose for years, even though I was witnessing to many other people, many of them strangers. I prayed about this, and one day I walked across the street and rang their doorbell. Both of them were at home, and cordially invited me in.

I started in right away before I lost my courage. "Aaron and Rose...I consider you as two of my close friends, and I just wanted to come over and tell you what happened to Floyd Eby spiritually. If I say something you don't like, just tell me and I will stop. Something has happened to Betty and me that has been tremendous, and I want to share it with you."

I proceeded to tell Aaron and Rose how, until recently, I had been a church goer, believing in parts of the Bible and not believing other parts of the Bible. Step by step, I went through God's Plan for my life, and how each step finally made sense to me. I would ask them if it made sense to them also. I just kept referring to myself, and my needs, and my beliefs, and how I had taken the necessary steps to actually join the Family of God. I proceeded to tell them how Betty and I, after taking these necessary steps to have a personal encounter with Jesus, found how and the need for getting closer and closer to God. What a wonderful, happy, fruitful life we were now having in Jesus with a guaranteed future. They agreed that this all made sense, and it had helped them see the real meaning of being a Christian and living a happy Christian life.

Many times since, I have witnessed to many close friends and relatives in this very same way. By just telling what has happened to me in detail, presenting the entire plan of God's salvation to my friends with no embarrassment, no insults, no holier than thou approach, no pressure, and in an environment of the love of Christ.

I don't even have to ask them if they have accepted Christ as personal Saviour.

If I am able to be used of God to bring them face to face with Him; if they haven't made a decision before, they have the opportunity at this time to accept Him, and certainly have understood the steps necessary.

God and my friends know if the decision has been sealed or not. And that is all that is necessary. As you follow up with them, your friends and God will reveal to you, through their lives, whether the decision was made.

A short time after this session with Aaron and Rose, we presented them a dignitary Bible at a large banquet. A few months later, I was a pall bearer at the funeral of my friend and brother in Christ, Aaron. I felt so good to know that Aaron's future had been guaranteed by our Lord, and he was now reaping his rewards. Also Rose had, and needed, God's Wonderful assurance at this time. Praise God that He gave me the courage in time -- His Wonderful Accepted Time.

A Letter Opens The Door

One day I met my friend, Ben, in the bank where he works. As we were chatting, Ben told me that he and his wife, Lottie, visited their son, Jud, at Oral Roberts University in Tulsa, Oklahoma.

Ben and Lottie and their family have been an outstanding family and fine citizens. Both boys played sports for me at Coldwater High School, and were excellent boys in many ways. A younger sister was born handicapped and God had used her to add much love to this family. It was a church going family.

The oldest boy, Joe, married a fine Christian girl, and Christianity really came alive in his life. As Ben related the story of his visit to Jud in Oklahoma, I had the feeling that Jud had had a personal encounter with Jesus.

I asked Ben for Jud's address, and I wrote him a letter, saying, "Jud, from a short conversation with your father in the bank the other day, I felt that you have come face to face with Jesus. What about it?"

I soon received an answer that recently he had accepted Jesus and had become "born again" as a child of God. His letter was thrilling as he related what had happened to him, and how our Lord has been changing his life.

God is now using Jud in many ways through the talents He gave him, especially his fine singing voice, which he is using to sing praises to His Lord.

One evening I called Ben and asked him if I could come over and chat with him and Lottie. I told him I had received a letter from Jud and would like to discuss it with them.

I read the letter to Ben and Lottie, and explained, "You know, if I had received a letter like this from my daughter a few years ago, I would have been astonished, amazed, and somewhat confused. Now I understand the meaning of such a letter, because the same thing happened to me that has happened to Jud."

Then I proceeded to tell them how I had come face to face with Jesus, and how since then Betty and I had disciplined ourselves to get close to God, and how God was blessing our lives. I also explained how we joined the Family of God through faith; and I explained each step. Ben and Lottie readily admitted that it made sense. They now attend one of our home Bible studies, and they attend church regularly. We have become close Christian friends, and we are growing spiritually together. I praise God for His Goodness!

Orders From The Preacher

One Sunday I had two services in two different churches -- one on the west side; the other on the northeast side of Detroit. The first one was at nine-thirty and the other at eleven in the morning, and there was travel time of about thirty-five minutes between churches.

I told the second pastor that I would have trouble making his service on time. He said it would be all right to come in a little late. Shortly after ten-thirty, I left the first church and headed for northeast Detroit. I arrived just after the singing had started, and the pastor was on the platform. An usher told me to go up to the platform and sit next to the pastor.

As I approached, the minister stepped down and instructed me to follow him. He led me into a small room at the front of the sanctuary, and started giving me some instructions.

I interrupted, "Just a minute, pastor, could we have a word of prayer first?"

He agreed, leading us in prayer, and then informed me, "We are not going to take an offering for the Gideons today. We know about the importance of the work and we will be sending the Gideons a good sized check. You can mention the Gideon work, but I know your background as a teacher and a coach, and I want you to present the Gospel to our young people."

I shortened the Gideon message, and then told the young people about Jesus. I ended with an invitation to anyone who wasn't sure that he was a child of God, that God had been speaking through me to them this morning, and I suggested that if they wanted for sure to get right with God, they should meet me in a room at the rear of the sanctuary.

Eight teenagers walked in, and I spent an hour with them, making friends with them, and going through the scriptures. Each one, including the preacher's daughter, made a decision to accept Jesus as personal Saviour, and joined the Family of God. I wrote to each one of them, telephoned, and visited several of them.

I asked the minister, "Certainly, Candy, your daughter, has professed Jesus before?"

"No," he answered. "We have been worried about her and these seven others also. Praise God!"

The orders from this preacher certainly were from God, because only God gives the increase.

* * *

Sometimes, It Takes Just One

One Sunday, I had three services in the same church in northern Michigan. I spoke in the morning, then to the youth in the late afternoon, and again at the evening service. At the end of the youth message, I gave an invitation to all who would like to get right with God for sure, to meet me in the room at the rear of the sanctuary.

After the message, I went to the room and stood at the door. People filed down the aisles leaving the church. It looked like God had not touched any teenager hearts. Finally, one boy quietly sided up to me, and right away I asked him if he would like to come in and talk with me. He nodded, and so we moved into the room.

As I presented him with a gift of two Bibles, three more boys came in. Soon they were followed by more boys and girls until twenty-five crowded in, wanting to get right with God.

This group of boys and girls have really enriched my spiritual life. I have received many letters, and personal pictures for my prayer board. I have also had the opportunity of visiting them again, and taking them for airplane rides, and calling them on the telephone. I surely love these new brothers and sisters in Christ.

Praise God for the one boy who had the courage to follow God's leading, and by his courage to step forth, led twenty-five others to come in to learn more about Jesus!

Coming To A Fanatic

We had a fine English teacher at our high school by the name of Eleanor, who during the term would have her students bring copies of the King James version of the Bible to class. She would have them read out of it for a week, because she liked the poetic style of this version.

However, I believed this was the only real interest she had in the Bible.

Although Eleanor and I were on friendly speaking terms, I understood from others that she thought I was a religious fanatic.

One morning Eleanor, who was married to one of our coaches, came to my home and asked to see me. I took her into my office, and asked her what I could do for her?

"You probably have heard that Paul and I are having trouble, and that he left me some months ago?"

I told her that I had heard something to that effect.

She continued. "For weeks, every day I have lived pretending that Paul would come back tomorrow, and this morning I found out that he is never coming back. I just don't know what I am going to do. I just can't stand it."

She started to cry intensely, and when she quieted down, I said, "Eleanor, why did you come to me? I know you have considered me somewhat of a Jesus fanatic."

"That is the reason I came to you. I realize you have something I need," she replied.

"Eleanor, I can't help you with your problems, but I can tell you about someone who can, Jesus Christ," I said.

After going through the scriptures and God's Plan for her life, she saw it made sense, and she professed Jesus.

"Now, Eleanor, since you are a child of God, if you will put Jesus first in your life, you can have a happy, fruitful life with or without Paul. Just commit you and your children to God, and get close to Him, and He will do the rest."

Sometime later, as I arrived home from a trip late at night, I had a letter from Eleanor, telling me that Paul was reunited with the family and they were happy. She now realized God's way is the right way.

God can use fanatics!

Turn Me Off

Recently at the Gideon International Convention in Washington, D.C., I met Chuck and his wife from Detroit with their seventeen year old son while they were checking into the hotel. I knew them well before this, and spent some time chatting with them, renewing an old friendship. Tom and I discussed athletics and other things of interest to him. The next morning I ran into the parents again, and they told me how Tom was rebelling against God. He had not wanted to come to the Convention, but upon the insistence of his parents, he had reluctantly decided to come. He had notified his parents, however, that he would not attend any of the meetings. I asked the parents if it would be all right to talk to Tom, and they quickly let me know that they hoped I would.

I walked out of one of the morning meetings and called my friend's room, knowing that the parents were in meetings and Tom would be sleeping in.

Tom answered the phone and I greeted him with, "Hey, Tom, this is Coach Eby. I bet I woke you up!"

"Yeh," he answered.

"Say, Tom, I had such a good time talking with you last night, I thought perhaps we could get together again this morning. What about meeting me down in the lobby at ten-thirty?"

He reluctantly agreed.

Tom got up immediately, dressed and came down to the meeting to see his parents. He wanted to know why they had put Coach Eby onto him. They told him I had asked permission to contact him. Tom's father then warned me about this turn of events.

When I met Tom in the lobby, I put my arm on his shoulder.

"Hey, friend, me meeting you again wasn't your parents' idea, it was my own bright idea. You see, Tom, I also used to have some bad hangups on Christianity. I just want a chance to tell you about them, and what happened to Coach Eby. I would like to talk to you in my room on one condition -- that if at any time you don't like what I am saying, you can tell me to turn off, and I will quit and leave. Isn't that fair enough?" I wanted to know. "You see, Tom," I added, "This condition puts you completely in control. Just a plain 'shut up' from you will immediately turn off the mouthiest guy in the state of Michigan. Isn't that something?"

Tom agreed this would be O.K.

We went to my room where Tom and I and our Lord settled

the hangups, and we came out of that room as good friends, and brothers in Christ.

I did not see Tom again during that Convention week, but his parents told me he went to the rest of the meetings. He asked his father at the end of the week how a person could become a Gideon. Praise Him for being a loving God.

Live The Life

I flew to an airport in southwestern Michigan one day to talk with two young ladies about Jesus. One was already saved and she wanted me to come and talk to her girl friend. Both of them had been married, and had many domestic problems -- they were now divorced.

As we three sat at a table in the airport building, and talked about the Bible and Jesus, a man and his wife walked in and purchased some pop from the pop machine. I waited for them to leave, but they didn't. In fact, both of them walked to our table where we had been reading and discussing the Bibles I had presented to these young ladies, Louise and Sally.

I made with some friendly chatter, praying that they would soon leave, but they didn't.

I decided perhaps I was to talk to them also about Jesus.

I began, and the man cut me short, "Listen, Mister, I know one of your former athletes, and every time I see him, which is too often, he is always quoting scriptures at me and shoving this crap down my throat. I am sick of it, and now I have to avoid him because, frankly, his life shows me nothing. I know he does things that I wouldn't think of doing, and if that is Christianity, I don't want anything to do with it."

I agreed with him that none of us has any right to preach to anyone. Each one of us has all he can do to keep his own relationship with Jesus where it should be, without judging another. This man and his wife listened while I told them how God had changed my life, and how I can only be a good example as Christ lives in me. The couple did not make a profession, but said that they would like to take the Bibles, and promised to read them.

Louise said she was surely surprised when the couple, with whom she was acquainted, came over and sat down when we had Bibles on the table and were talking about the Lord. Louise said that previously this couple would leave immediately if anyone so much as mentioned the Bible or Jesus.

Sally accepted the Lord and joined the Family of God as we closed the session.

Let us pray to our Saviour to help us live a life pleasing to Him, so we will not be a stumbling block to someone else's salvation. Praise God for His strength. Philippians 4:13 *I can do all things through Christ which strengtheneth me.*

The Doctor And His Wife

Through some speaking engagements, I became a close friend of a doctor and his wife. One night I received a phone call from Doctor Dan.

"Floyd, we have a daughter who married a doctor, and he is now finishing his training at Michigan State. Even though our daughter, Tina, was brought up in a Christian home, we don't believe she is a Christian or her husband either, although they are both grand people. We feel that you are the Lord's man to talk to them. Would you?"

I told Doctor Dan I would only promise one thing. I would try to make contact. The rest would be up to God, Dr. Wayne and Tina. Doctor Dan gave me their telephone number. I rang, and when Doctor Wayne answered I introduced myself as well as I could over the phone. I asked him where he was from, and where he went to school. Fortunately, he had gone to high school and college where I knew the coaches. Doctor Wayne had been a football player so this gave us a common interest. After chatting with him for awhile, I asked him if I could talk with his wife, Tina. After trying to make friends with Tina over the phone, I asked her if I could visit them, and she said it would be all right.

I said, "You know, Tina, I am flying to Howell next Tuesday to speak at a night meeting, and I could fly up early and meet you before I fly on to Howell."

She agreed to meet me at the East Lansing airport. Tina was teaching school at East Lansing and would pick me up after school. Doctor Wayne would be home a little later.

Tuesday afternoon, Tina was at the airport to meet me and drove me to their apartment. I gave her a couple of Bibles and started to tell her why I now believe the Bible even though I didn't at one time. I was over halfway through the plan of salvation when her husband walked in.

I immediately went to him. "Doctor Wayne," I said. "I am Coach Eby, the man who talked to you on the phone the other night. I have just been talking to Tina about a tremendous new way of life my wife and I have found. It is so great, I just want to include you in on this rap session, O.K.?"

I gave him a couple of Bibles with his name written in them and my name and address also. I said, "Tina, if it is O.K. with you, I will start from the beginning so Wayne won't miss a thing. Is that all right?"

She assured me that it was.

I presented what had happened to Floyd Eby, and how each step made sense to me, and they both agreed that it also made sense to them. They both professed to believe, and I knew at least the seed had been sown. The rest was up to God, the Holy Spirit, and Doctor Wayne and Tina.

The following week they drove to Grand Rapids with Tina's parents to hear me speak, and I had a short chat with them. God gradually worked in their lives, and now Tina is on fire for Jesus. Doctor Wayne is getting closer and now they have a beautiful baby daughter to bring up in the nurture and admonition of the Lord. I praise God for what He can do when seed is sown on fertile ground!

Teenage Rebellion

Some Christian friends referred their own son, Doug to me. He was going to school in Detroit. He had rebelled against God and his Christian parents. I wrote to Doug and introduced myself, telling him about my background and my acquaintance with his parents. In the letter I told him that he sounded like the kind of guy I would like to know and visit. I included a self-addressed, stamped envelope, and asked him to write back and let me know if he was interested. I promised I would not preach to him, but just discuss something good that had happened to me. For a long time I didn't hear from Doug, but after I had given up, I received a letter from him telling me that he had many problems and would like to see me. I wrote back and told him I was going to speak at a certain church in Detroit on Sunday. If he would like to meet me there, I would take him out to dinner and we could have a rap session while we were eating.

I did not receive an answer.

When I went to Detroit for this speaking engagement, I took two young Christian men with me. They were in their twenties, and were close friends.

After the message, I walked to the back of the church to greet the people as they came out of the sanctuary. I shook hands with a young man and asked how he was, and he answered, "I am Doug." I had not known that he was in the congregation. I introduced Doug to my friends, Mike and Bill, and the four of us went to a nearby restaurant for dinner. Doug and I took a separate table from Mike and Bill, so Doug would feel free to talk. Doug told me about all of his serious problems and I told him about Jesus. How He could take over all of the problems, and how Doug could join the Family of God just like Coach Eby had.

We had a good, long discussion and then Mike and Bill were able to give their testimonies to Doug.

Two nights later I received a telephone call from Doug's parents, and they told me Doug had called from Detroit that same Sunday night. Doug had told them about hearing Coach Eby speak, about our dinner together, and about our discussion of the Bible and Jesus.

Also he told them he had gone back to his apartment that night, got down on his knees, and accepted Jesus as Saviour and joined the Family of God.

Doug is still having some problems getting close to God to

surrender his life to him, but he is making progress. God is waiting patiently for that real commitment from Doug so he can continue to bless him in many more ways. I praise God that He is a patient God!

Cold Turkey

After speaking in a large church near Pontiac, Michigan, a young man came up to me at the rear of the sanctuary. He said, "You sound like a man who likes to go around telling people about Jesus."

"I do only if God opens the door," I answered cautiously. "I am completely helpless and ineffective if God hasn't prepared the way."

"Would you go to see my wife? We are separated and she has our two children. She has a boy friend. He is there right now. I saw his car when I came to church. Both of them sure need Jesus," he said.

I asked him where she lived, and he told me about four miles from the church. I told him that I didn't have a car, and I would need a ride to the Oakland airport later where I would go to fly my plane home. This young man told me he would take me to his wife, but he wouldn't dare stay. I told him I would rather not have him drive me there. He gave me the address, her name and the boy friend's name, and I told him I would only promise that I would try to make contact. The rest would be up to God and Cathy.

I recruited a man from the church who took his wife home and then came back and took me to Cathy's house. He said he would wait for me and then take me to the airport. As I got out of the car at Cathy's house, I told my driver friend, that if God hadn't preceded me, I would be back in forty seconds or less. If God had prepared the way, it would be at least forty-five minutes.

I walked to the front door with a couple of Bibles in my hand, and pushed the door bell. A young lady opened the door. "Are you Cathy?" I asked. She nodded. "I am Coach Eby from Coldwater, Michigan. I am no preacher, but I have just had a service at a nearby church. I wonder if you have a little time, and if I could chat with you?"

"What do you want, and what about?" She asked.

"That is a good question. I will give you the answer. I want to tell you about a new way of life that my wife and I have been living recently that is just tremendous. A real exciting way of living that beats anything anybody can find, and the cost is right, because it is free. I can hardly wait until I have a chance to tell you about it. Wouldn't you like to hear about it? There is no obligation. And you can tell me to shut up any time you want to, and I will leave. What about it?"

Cathy said, "Come on in."

I sat down in a chair near the door, and she sat down on the sofa across the room. I said, "Is Ray here? Perhaps he would like to listen to it also."

Cathy said she would go into the other room and ask him. Soon she came back with Ray following and he sat down in a chair. I gave them both two Bibles, each as gifts with their names in them. I opened the scriptures, and started talking about the Bible and Jesus. I sensed right away that Cathy was prepared, but Ray wasn't. I concentrated on Cathy and asked her to read the verses and answer the questions. It all made sense to Cathy, and she professed Jesus as Saviour and joined the Family of God, while Ray hardly said a word. He did bow his head when I asked God's blessing on Cathy's decision and on her children.

I haven't been able to contact Cathy since, and my letter remains unanswered. I know Cathy was sincere in her decision, but you know the devil is still around. Perhaps he is using Ray to keep Cathy from growing spiritually. In spite of the devil, I know God is in control, and I praise Him for this!

But Jesus beheld them, and said unto them,
With men this is impossible;
but with God all things are possible
Matthew 19:26

13

GOD IS ABLE

God Never Makes A Mistake

Two years ago I was speaking to a group of teenagers in
Houston, Texas. As I finished the message, six teenagers
came to me and one of them said, "Mr. Eby, we would like to
talk to you about this Jesus you have been telling us about."
"Great," I answered. "Come into this room, and we will
have a rap session."
After they were seated, I presented each one of them with a
testament, asking each his name, address, telephone number,
age, and grade. I chatted with each one personally, making
friends, before I started on the necessary steps of salvation.
The first four were from four different states. Then I came to
the fifth one, "What is you name, young man?" He answered
in Spanish. I cannot understand Spanish, but I knew he was
speaking in that language.
I immediately drew back and meditated with my Lord.
"God, I know that you never make a mistake. But I have to
tell you someone surely 'flubbed up' here. You must know

I cannot speak or understand Spanish. There is just no way you can use Floyd Eby to communicate your wonderful plan for this young man's life. Why did you send him here? All he is going to be is a bottleneck to these other five young people." After I finished telling my Lord off, I did the same thing that any of you would have done. I skipped him and went to the sixth teenager.

"Chum, what is your name?"

"Don."

"Where are you from, Don?"

"Puerto Rico."

"You speak good English, Don."

"I speak good Spanish also, Sir," he countered.

You see, friends, God doesn't ever make a mistake. When he sent six teenagers to me who needed to have a personal encounter with Jesus; He knew that one of them only spoke Spanish. He knew that I could only speak English, so He sent another teenager who also needed to come face to face with Jesus, but could also be used as an interpreter.

As I went around each one of the group going over the necessary beliefs, I came to Don from Puerto Rico with this question, "Don, do you really believe that Jesus, God upon this earth, went to the cross, and died for your sins and my sins? Do you actually believe it, accept it, and receive it unto yourself in faith? Do you, friend?"

"I do, I really do," He replied.

"Then ask our buddy from Mexico this same question," I urged.

So Don rambled off some Spanish which I couldn't understand, but I knew what he was asking him. I had no trouble understanding Dave's answer as he clenched both fists, held them up and brought them both down at the same time three distinct times as he said, "Yeh, yeh, yeh."

I praise God that you and I serve a God who never makes a mistake.

After arriving back home, I wrote a letter to Dave, and three weeks later I received an answer in Spanish. I had our high school Spanish teacher interpret it for me. Dave started the

GOD IS ABLE / 193

letter, "Dear friend and brother in the Lord Jesus Christ." It sounded like the Apostle Paul starting a letter; it indicated that Dave had been reading the Bible. In his first letter, Dave indicated that his interpreter of my first letter was an unbeliever, so the next letter I wrote in English I witnessed to the interpreter. Dave told me that when the interpreter brought the second letter to him, that he and his parents witnessed to him. Dave said he didn't make a profession, but they were going to pray for him until he did. Doesn't God work in marvelous ways? A year later Dave coaxed his parents to let him visit his Aunt and Uncle in Toledo, Ohio, so he could also visit me. I flew to Toledo and picked up Dave and his cousin and flew them to Coldwater where they spent two days with me. We were able to use Dave's cousin as an interpreter. I am so thankful that we have such a Great and Able God!

God, The Great Psychiatrist

The brother of Kitty asked me to visit her in the state mental hospital in Kalamazoo. As I took her into a private room, you could tell that she was mentally disturbed and depressed. Kitty was a former student of mine, and remembered me. Even though she was in a bad mental state, I opened the Bible and told her about God's compassion and love for her; also how she, in a simple way, could join the Family of God, and God could then help her and bless her. Step by step we took up God's Plan of Salvation, and she understood and accepted Jesus as her personal Saviour and became my sister in Christ.

Six weeks later, Kitty was discharged from the mental institution, and has never been back. And that has been over three years ago. I also had the privilege of baptizing Kitty upon her request. I praise God that He is the greatest psychiatrist of all.

Because I Love Jesus

Jake was an alcoholic of many years. His eyesight was bad

and the only time he drove was when he was drunk, and didn't know any better.

Because of his eyesight, he could not obtain a driver's license. I took his son home one night, and met Jake and Flora, the parents, and God opened the door for me to talk to both of them about Jesus. Both of them accepted Christ and became my brother and sister in Christ. They started attending a home Bible study each week and they began to grow spiritually.

However, Jake was still having trouble with alcohol. He would be dry all week, and then on Friday -- pay day at the shop -- his drinking buddies would come around with the usual invitation. "Come on, Jake, this is pay day, let's go out and get soused."

Jake would tell them he couldn't, and his buddies would ask him why he didn't want to go drinking with them any more. He would make excuses like he had to go shopping with his wife, or fix something at home; but eventually he would give in and go drinking with them.

One weekend I received a call that Jake was drunk and was beating his wife, Flora.

I drove to their house and tried to stop him. He was still beating her severely. After I interceded, he went into a bedroom and came out with a loaded shotgun. He pointed the gun at my head, started cursing me, using obscene language.

"Eby, I am going to blow your head off."

I really thought he was going to pull the trigger, because I knew he didn't know what he was doing.

"Jake," I said quietly, "If you pull that trigger, I am so big you can't miss me, and you will kill me. I will go to Heaven, and you will go to jail, and that is no bargain for you."

He glared at me with his gun pointed at my head, and I thought for sure he was going to pull the trigger. Finally he lowered the gun and took it back into the bedroom and I left.

Three weeks later, after Flora had told him what he had done, he apologized to me. He came to Bible study, and announced, "Coach, God has taken the alcohol from me. I know for sure this time."

I thought to myself, I had heard that before. I remembered how Jake would break down and cry as he asked me why God wouldn't take this from him and give him a happy, fruitful life. I could only answer, "I don't know, Jake. Perhaps He is going to make you pay a price. I just don't know."

However, all I said when he told me that God had taken it from him was, "What makes you think so, Jake?"

"Because three weeks ago on Friday, my drinking buddies came to me as usual, and asked me to go with them. I started making the same silly excuses. Then I realized these excuses had never worked. When they asked me why I wouldn't go with them, this time I stood up and shouted, 'Because I love Jesus.' They left and haven't bothered me since." Jake hasn't had a drink for over two and a half years. I praise God that He will help us with any problem if we put Him first and give Him the Glory!

A Wonderful Miracle

Larry was one of my former students and football players. He was not a football player very long because he would not follow the training rules. He gradually became worse and worse until he committed every wrong in the book. He was an alcoholic, embezzler, thief, sponger, con man, and you name it. Larry had a good personality and a sharp mind, but he used both of these assets to do wrong. Larry has been in seven different prisons in the United States, several times in several specific prisons. Many times while in the Army he went AWOL, and spent much time in the guardhouse. He lied about everything and anything; in fact, he could almost convince you that telling the truth was a sin. Larry would borrow money from some gullible person on the pretense of going into some new business that was going to make a fortune. Then he would go to a bar and buy drinks for everyone, playing the "big shot" with someone else's money. Then he would laugh about it. Larry would embezzle money where he worked, and was clever enough to blame it on some innocent person, and he would laugh when they got fired.

Adultery became a top favorite with Larry.

One night Larry came to my house and wanted to talk with me. I knew he was going to try to wheedle some more money out of me. We went down into my basement recreation room, and he started talking to me about the Bible. "Coach, is God all powerful? Does God know everything? Does God know the future? Is God always right?" I answered all his questions in the affirmative.

"Then God knew before I was born that I was destined for hell, and whatever I do doesn't make any difference, because my fate had been determined before I was even born."

"You are all wrong, Larry," I answered. "The fact that God knows all things doesn't prevent you from accepting Jesus as Saviour right now through faith. He has promised through His Holy Inspired Word that anyone can come to Him at any time just as they are, and God doesn't lie, so Larry don't blame God for your weakness and problems."

Larry kept searching for the answer, and one night called me and asked me to come over.

After going through the Bible with Larry about God's Plan for his life, Larry and I both got down on our knees, and Larry invited Jesus into his life. His life didn't change all at once, but I am happy to be able to tell you that Larry has not had a drink for over a year.

He went back to school even though he was in his forties. He now has an excellent job, working with alcoholics. He is helping them to straighten out their lives, believing that God is able to help any and all alcoholics.

Certainly, God performed a real miracle in Larry's life. God can and will do the same for anyone who is willing to surrender his life to Jesus!

God Will Provide

I was helping to organize and train members in a new Gideon Camp in Petoskey, Michigan. We invited prospects to a dinner meeting and signed up eight members and their wives. I stayed overnight in a Petoskey motel. Since it was my responsibility, under God, to select and appoint the new camp officers for the eight month training program, I spent much time in prayer that night over names of the new members, many of whom I had never met before that night. It seemed like I spent most of the night praying that our Lord would lead me to the right name for president of the camp.

Mentally, I went through the list of those eight men, and each time I would ask God to point out the one He would have as president. God seemed to be pointing me to Dennis. But I knew about Dennis, and could not see him as president.

I rolled out of bed, got on my knees, prayed again, then got back into bed. But once again I stopped at Dennis' name. I spent several hours doing this, and finally I told the Lord, "You know it can't be Dennis, Lord. Don't you know that Dennis and his wife have eight children; that the oldest is thirteen? How could his wife be active at all? Also, Lord, don't you know that Dennis goes to work every morning at three-thirty, and doesn't finish generally until ten o'clock? There is just no way that he can be president."

But the Lord would not point out any other name for president.

Several days later I called Dennis. He lived about fifty miles from Petoskey.

"Dennis, this is Floyd Eby from Coldwater, and I have been praying to God that He would select the right man for president of this new camp. God continues to lead me to you. Do you know of any reason why the Lord wouldn't have you?"

Dennis said he guessed not.

So, Dennis became president -- for a three year term. He was used greatly of God in this Missionary Arm of his Church. And his wife, Dorothy, was also interested and active. You say, how can this be? Because we have a great God and One who never makes a mistake. You see, no sooner had Dennis become president, when God gave him a much better job -- and with the necessary time to spend on this ministry.

Praise a God who is not limited to what He can do!

God Can Change Priorities

I was visiting a Michigan Gideon Camp one night when I was state president, and the zone leader, Ted, was conducting the annual election. A man named Peter was nominated for the office of president, and immediately Peter stood and said, "I love my Lord Jesus, and I love this Missionary Arm of my Church, but we need to accept reality. With my schedule as a coach and teacher, there is no way during the next seven months that I can make one weekly prayer meeting or one monthly camp meeting. Wouldn't it be foolish to have a president who cannot possibly attend meetings?"

I stood up and asked the zone leader, Ted, if I could say a word.

Peter started to sit down, and I said, "No, Peter, please remain standing. I just want to ask you one question. Are you willing to let Jesus make the decision about your schedule, time, and how He wants to use you, or are you going to insist in making the decision yourself?"

"As long as you put it that way," Peter answered, "I will say no more."

Peter was elected president, and six months later, when I was visiting this same camp he gave a testimony. "You know, I have never been busier than this year at school, but our Lord has made it possible for me to attend every weekly prayer meeting and every monthly camp meeting, and my school responsibilities have not suffered."

Peter was president for three years, and God used him as a real leader. Oh, how I praise a God who can rearrange priorities and schedules so we can do His work, and receive a real blessing!

God Uses A Snow Storm

One night I drove to St. Johns, Michigan, for a speaking engagement, and my plan was to drive back to Michigan State University that same night and stay overnight for a cabinet meeting on Saturday. Then I planned to drive to Bay City on Saturday night for another speaking engagement, and then back to my home on Saturday night. After the meeting at St. Johns, I drove to East Lansing through a heavy snow storm. The next morning, the entire state was immobilized with one of the worst snowstorms in history.

Naturally, our cabinet meeting, as well as my speaking engagement for that night in Bay City had to be called off.

Radio and television broadcasts warned people to stay where they were and not to try the roads.

After dinner I thought, if I took my time, I could make it to Coldwater where I had a Sunday speaking engagement. So, I started out at ten to fifteen miles per hour, trying to stay in the middle of the freeway. You could not tell where the pavement ended and the ditch began. Cars by the hundreds had been abandoned where they had slipped off into the ditch. I was particularly careful, barely creeping along. When I couldn't see through the blowing snow, I would come to a complete stop, and wait until I could see better. As I neared the Olivet exit on I-69, I slowly passed a car that had slid into the ditch. It looked like it was loaded with children and women with no man present.

I stopped in the middle of the freeway, got out, and went to the car. The woman driver had six children with her. I asked if I could help. I tried, but I could not budge the car from the ditch. So, I asked this family to pile into my car, so I could take them to my home in Coldwater. They lived in northern Indiana, just across the state line from my hometown. The mother, Bonnie, refused to do this because she wanted to stay with the car. She wanted me to send a wrecker. Finally, she did decide to send the two oldest girls with me, so they could bring a wrecker back. The two girls and I drove off in my car.

At each exit, the girls, Sally and Jean, insisted I drive off on a side road to a nearby town to find a wrecker. I was sure we would also get stuck, and would be in the same predicament as the others, and with no chance of helping them.

However, the girls were getting more anxious and hysterical, so finally when I reached the I-94 exit, I made my bid to get help. We, too, slipped into the ditch, and were stuck.

I showed Sally and Jean how to start the car and turn the heater on when they got cold. I told them I would be back with a wrecker as soon as possible, and not to worry. I started climbing snowdrifts, and walking the best I could until I reached I-94. I was able to catch a ride with a jeep to U.S. 27 where I found a wrecker. However, the owner of the wrecker wasn't about to go out on another job. He had been working for about twenty hours straight, and he was dead tired. He had two more jobs, he said, and then he was going home to sleep. Then he recognized me as the former Coach of Coldwater High School. He had played against my teams. He agreed that if I would go with him on the next two jobs, he would pull me out before he went home.

Two hours later, as we were trying to get the wrecker to my car, sheriff deputies on snowmobiles told us there was no chance of us reaching the car. I told the deputies that there were a couple of teenagers in my car and I was concerned about them.

The deputies said they had already picked them up and had transported them by snowmobile to Marshall High School. They would also take me there where stranded people were staying overnight. I then had my first snowmobile ride. I asked the driver how fast we were going, and he said thirty miles an hour. I would have sworn we were going ninety.

I had left my glasses in the car, and upon arriving at Marshall High School, I started to look for Sally and Jean. I didn't even know their names at that time, and I could just vaguely remember what they looked like. Without my glasses, it was like looking for a needle in a haystack.

There were hundreds of people in the high school. Every time I saw two girls, I asked them if they were from Butler, Indiana, as this was about all I knew about the girls. I must have looked for an hour until the girls located me. They had been down in the gym. They were glad to see me, but they were really worried about their mother, brothers and sisters. The people in charge of this temporary shelter, including the athletic director, Jay and his wife, were school people and personal friends of mine. I was able to use a phone, and I called the sheriff's department in Olivet. But they had no news, and had not located the girls' family. I described the location as best I could and asked them to send snowmobiles to get them.

I reminded the sheriff they had been there a long time and were undoubtedly suffering from the cold.

Twice more I called, and still no news. The girls were once more crying and hysterical.

I went over to a dark corner, got on my knees and opened my heart to God. I asked for help for these new friends of mine. I went back to Sally and Jean and told them that everyone would now be all right. I had gone to my Lord in prayer and asked for a definite answer. I called again and the family had been located and brought in by snowmobiles to Olivet College.

Jay and his wife invited me and the girls to come to their house and spend the rest of the night. The next morning I called my wife, and a Christian friend drove my van bus from Coldwater to pick us up. We drove on to Olivet College, and found the rest of the girls' family, and brought them to my home in Coldwater. We were then able to contact the husband and father, and after several hours at our house, the family was on their way home to Indiana.

God didn't at the time open the door for me to witness to them. I told them that if they would write me a letter, I would send each one a present.

Jean wrote back to me, and I sent a personal worker's testament to her with her name in it. My name, address, and telephone number were inscribed also. Eventually, I received a letter from each one, and I returned a new testament to each. Jean and I started corresponding regularly. She was a junior in high school, and I started telling her about Jesus in my letters.

Several months later, I had the opportunity to see the family again. I had to fly to Traverse City to speak on a Friday night; stay overnight, fly to Chicago to speak at a banquet Saturday night, stay overnight, and speak in a Chicago church on Sunday. This gave me the opportunity on the way back to land at Syracuse, Indiana. So I met my snowbound friends, including Orlin, Bonnie, Sally and her husband Willy, Jean,

Kitty, Craig, Eric and Lou.

I opened up the scriptures to all nine of them that Sunday afternoon in their mobile home. I explained how each of them could join the Family of God by accepting Jesus, through faith. Eight became my brothers and sisters in Christ. Only Bonnie's husband, Orlin, would not accept Jesus. We are all still praying for him. I have visited and corresponded with the family for some time. I thank God as I see them come closer to God, and as I see them growing spiritually.

One night I received a telephone call from Sally.

"Coach, I wish you would talk with Willy," she said. "I want you to tell him where he is all wrong. He is just terrible with some of the things he is doing. He isn't acting like a Christian at all. Will you speak to him on the phone and tell him off?" She was mad, and obviously upset.

"No, Sally," I answered. "I won't tell Willy off, or say whether either one of you is right. If Willy would like to, I would be happy to speak to him on the phone."

Willy came to the phone.

"Coach, I don't know really what has happened to me. I haven't smoked or cussed since I became a Christian. But last night Sally made me mad, and I lit up and blew smoke in her face, and I cussed her up one side and down the other. We have had a real knock down. Now I don't know what to do."

"Listen, Willy," I said. "This is no big deal. God can soon straighten it out. I want you to hang up on me, take the Bible, and you and Sally read it together -- now. Then get on your knees together, and take all of this to our Lord. Goodnight, friend."

I hung up.

Three days later I received a nice letter from Sally stating that everything was now all right.

I praise God for being the greatest of all marriage counselors.

Get Out Of The Way, God

While weighing 287 pounds, I was sitting in my doctor's

office with sugar diabetes; my blood sugar was 316, and I was going blind. I had first noticed my problem flying my plane. I could no longer read the instruments, I told the doctor. He exploded.

"Listen, Coach, I am getting sick and tired of you fat people eating yourself into sugar diabetes, going blind, losing your limbs, and even dying. Either you are going to lose weight, stick to my rules, and do as I say, or I will drop you like a hot potato. You are now grounded, and if I give you just one shot of insulin, you are through flying forever. That's the regulation. I am going to pull you right out of your job, and slap you right into the hospital. We don't even have a room for you, so you will have to lay on a cot in the hallway."

"Listen, Doc," I pleaded. "You can't pull me off my job. I work for the Lord."

"I don't care who you work for," he snapped back.

"No way, Doc, are you going to put me in the hallway of that hospital," I stated. "I know everyone in town, and to every person who comes down that hallway, I would have to explain what is wrong with me. Can you think of anything worse than being faced with that?"

"Then you will listen to me, Coach, and do as I say," he insisted. "You know if you can whip this diabetes with diet alone, perhaps you can fly again. If you have to use insulin, you are all through flying. Now, let's get down to the necessary rules."

The doctor put me on a 1,000 calorie per day diet, a weekly fasting blood sugar test, and a weekly doctor's appointment with a weigh-in ceremony. My wife threw away her recipe books; bought a gram scale, learned to substitute foods, and once again, how to pack lunches.

I took the entire situation to the Lord.

"Lord, you know I have run the diet gamut before, and have never been successful -- only on a temporary basis. I am admitting to you right now that I cannot do what the doctor wants me to do, and what I need to do. If you want me to continue working for you, then you are going to have to take over. I am committing it all into your hands, and I am not going to be concerned about it at all. It is your baby -- so there, Lord. What do you think about that?"

For the next nine months, it was selected amounts of food, fasting blood sugar tests, doctor appointments, and the carrying of sack lunches whenever I traveled for speaking engagements.

One night I was speaking at a large gathering at the Holiday Inn in Gaylord, Michigan. I explained to the manager that because I was on a strict diet prescribed by my family physician, I had to eat a sack lunch. All foods had to be weighed and cooked a certain way. The manager said that would be all right. As the rest of the people were eating their sumptuous meal, I pulled out my sack and started eating my carrots and celery.

In walked the manager, who exclaimed, "Look at this folks, I have now seen everything."

He pointed at me. "Here's a man who flies up here in his own plane, and is too cheap to buy a dinner."

Of course, he got the laugh he expected. But I got a laugh, too. "Lynn, you are a poor loser," I said. "You are just mad that our group doesn't use your bar, and you are losing money."

He agreed.

Because I had turned my diet problem over to the Lord, I lost eighty pounds in nine months, and I wasn't even hungry. My blood sugar returned to normal, and my eyesight returned as my weight went down. For awhile, pilot friends made trips with me, until the doctor released me to fly by myself again. Everything had turned out just great, and I gave the Lord the Glory. Then, one day, I told the Lord, "Get out of my way, now, God. I will take over and make the decisions." Since that day, I have been hungry and have found it more difficult to lose ten pounds than it was to lose the eighty. I praise God because He has kept my weight stable for the last three years. Oh, how I wish I could learn to turn all my problems over to Jesus and leave them there all of the time. I am so thankful for a concerned God!

*　*　*

The Coach Couldn't Change Him

As head basketball coach at Coldwater High School, I had instituted an intensive basketball program from the fifth grade on up. Each Saturday, the lower grades were divided into different teams, and coached by some of my varsity and junior varsity players, they would play regular games in the gym.

One Saturday morning, as usual, I was watching the competition. In one game I noticed a tall, gangling, left-handed boy who seemed to be better than the rest. I pulled him out of the game, took him upstairs to my office, weighed him, checked his height and asked his age; obtained his name and his parents' names, and address. I then sent Gordon back to his game.

I jumped into the car and drove to Gordon's home, and introduced myself to his parents. I asked them their ages, and weight, and then left for home.

I took out my books and charts, and determined that Gordon would be six foot, three inches tall when he would play on my varsity as a junior. I always prided myself on the fact that if I could get a boy young enough, I could develop not only his basketball abilities, but also his attitude, character, and emotional stability. So my other coaches and I worked with Gordon for five years, and sure enough he grew to six feet, three inches in height, and was on my varsity as a junior.

However, instead of being a star and leading us to a championship, Gordon could not make the starting five. He was relegated to sixth spot. Even as a senior, and after several of the first five had graduated, Gordon was still sixth man. He had all of the physical abilities to be a star, but he was not coachable. If I said to him, "Gordon, you are making that pivot wrong. I want you to do it this way." He would nod, but I knew deep down inside, he was thinking, "I wish that stupid coach would get off my back. I know how this game should be played."

Gordon would swear in the locker room when I wasn't around, and he would give his opponent an elbow if the official wasn't watching. He didn't do anything serious enough to be released from the team, but he was uncoachable. During Gordon's senior year, after the basketball season, he started reading the Bible and became a child of God. About a week after he was saved, I was officiating a church league basketball game in which Gordon was playing. Even though I knew he had been saved the week before, I somehow dreaded this game. I knew I no longer had any influence over Gordon; as the regular basketball season was over, and I was afraid he would revert back to the old meanness. I just didn't think God could change him overnight.

But God had.

I had wonderful Christian fellowship with Gordon during that game. I have had such fellowship with him ever since.

Gordon is now teaching in a nearby high school. He sponsors school Bible clubs, and goes out and talks to people about Jesus. I am so happy that he is my brother in Christ. Praise God that He can change people even though Coach Eby can't.

God's Timing Is Perfect

During a crusade in the thumb area of Michigan, I was visiting some homes that were referrals and I came to a house where the referring person had said, "Stop here only if you run out of other calls, because it will probably do no good."

I had only a few minutes left before the meeting was to start, so I stopped and knocked at the door.

The young lady who opened the door, stepped out on the porch. I introduced myself. "I am Coach Eby from Coldwater, Michigan, and I am having meetings at a local church. I thought I would stop in to say hello and see if you have any problems."

Jackie answered, "I have all kinds of problems. I have just now been praying that God would send a messenger to help me, and I have been expecting you."

Of course, I had not known her before. I asked her if I could come out after the meeting and visit with her and her husband. She said he would be home, and she would like that even though she didn't know how her husband would feel about it.

After the meeting, I took a fine young Christian man with me, and drove out to Jackie's house about ten o'clock. Jackie let us in, but her husband had called from the tavern to say he wouldn't be home for some time. Jackie has ten children, all home except one.

I opened the Bible, after presenting Jackie with two Bibles, and introduced Jackie to Jesus. Wiping the tears from her eyes, Jackie professed Jesus as Saviour and joined the Family of God. We closed in prayer asking God's blessing on her family, and especially on this new sister in Christ.

I have visited Jackie, corresponded with her, and called her several times. Each time I contact her, she has a pressing need at that very time. Her husband is still not saved, and Jackie desperately needs Christian fellowship. Praise God His timing is perfect.

Just Good Enough To Make It

I had been praying for one of my former athletes, one of the most outstanding ones that I had coached. One night I called Hal, and asked him if he and his wife were going to be home. He checked with his wife and then said, "Yes." I asked him what time his children went to bed and he replied about a quarter after nine. I told him I would be over a little after that. Hal was on the defensive from the beginning of our visit.

"Coach, I know I haven't been going to church very often, but I talk and think about God a lot. Even when my friend, Rex, and I go hunting we discuss God."

"I am not here, Hal, to discuss your church attendance," I interrupted. "But what is your relationship with the Lord Jesus?"

"What do you mean?" he asked.

"I mean where would you go if you died tonight?"

"Well, I think I would go to Heaven," he countered.

"What makes you think so, Hal?"

"Well, Coach, I go to church sometimes; I live a pretty decent life, I support my family, and I think I am just about good enough to make it."

I then asked Hal if he wouldn't like to know for sure that he would go to Heaven. He wanted to know if that was possible to know for sure. I assured him it was, and I opened the Bible and had him read the salvation verses. Hal became my brother in Christ, and he and his wife, Pam have brought up a fine Christian family. Praise God that He can make us know for sure!

Twenty-Twenty Spiritual Vision

After finishing a message in a large Detroit church, I stepped down from the platform, and noticed a lady leading a teenager up the aisle to see me. She said, "Mr. Eby, this is my daughter, Yvonne, and she would like to speak to you." I grabbed Yvonne's hand and said, "I am Coach Eby from Coldwater, and I am so happy to meet you. How are you, anyway?" She told me how thrilled she was to hear about the Gideon Missionary Arm of her church. Yvonne loved the testimonies I gave about those who are being won to her precious Jesus through the distribution of His Word. Yvonne is totally blind. She was born prematurely, and placed in an oxygen tent where she was given too much oxygen, and it destroyed her eyesight. She has never been able to see. Yvonne and I and her mother, Marcia, became well acquainted that day, and three days later I received a letter from Yvonne. She wrote, "I praise God for being blind, because I am sure that I can see better spiritually because of my blindness. You know, Brother Eby, there are people walking around in Coldwater and Detroit with twenty-twenty eyesight who are stumbling around in darkness, because they are not walking in the light like you and me."

Over the past several years, Yvonne and I have become close friends. The second time I met Yvonne, after much correspondence and many phone calls, was at Western University at Kalamazoo, where she is a student. I called to tell her I was going to come over to see her and take her out to dinner, and she answered, "Fantastic." As I located her dormitory, I asked the desk to notify her that I was there. Down the stairs, cane and all, came Yvonne.

I rushed to her and shook her hand, and told her how glad I was to see her again.

She answered, "Say, you have lost a lot of weight."

"How did you know, Yvonne?" I exclaimed.

"Your hand is not nearly as plump as it was eight months ago," she informed me.

After eating, and after much discussion about our Jesus, I took Yvonne back to the dormitory. "You brought me to the wrong dormitory," she informed me.

"How do you know, Yvonne?"

"Because I have been here before. My dormitory is the next one east of here."

She guided me to the correct one.

Yvonne has been a great source of encouragement to me with her dedication to our Jesus. She has flown with me several times, and has participated in several of my crusades. God has given Yvonne a beautiful voice, and He touches the hearts of many people, as Yvonne sings praises to His Glory as she reads the music in braille. Yvonne's dedication to Jesus is not limited to her singing. For several years she gave back to Jesus one-half of her allowance to buy Bibles to send overseas to tell others about her precious Jesus. Recently I have been able to record Yvonne's talent for television.

I praise my God that He can make the blind to see, because Yvonne sees all of the important things of this world.

Counseling People With Problems

I praise God that I have finally learned that I cannot help people with their problems.

Only Jesus can do this.

Therefore, I ask the people I am counseling not to tell me their problems because I cannot help them. But I tell them I will gladly introduce them to One who can.

210 / CALLING GOD'S TOWER...COME IN, PLEASE!

The only effective counseling I can offer is to give a person an opportunity to join the Family of God; then continue to encourage them to grow spiritually, or get close to God, or get to know Him better, and better, or become a real close friend of Jesus, or increase their faith. If they follow this advice, and live by it regularly and consistently, then God will change their lives and the problems will be shouldered by Jesus.

They are God's servants, not yours.
They are responsible to Him, not to you. Let Him
tell them whether they are right or wrong. And God
is able to make them do as they should
Romans 14:4 Living Bible

14

ONLY GOD CHANGES PEOPLE

You Know What?

I was referred to a young lady named Amy. I recognized her as one of my former students as she opened the door.

"Hi, Coach," she said.

By the time she was twenty three, Amy had been married twice, and recently had been living with a boy friend.

She was the mother of five children by these three different men. Amy was willing to listen, and after reading God's Word, and going through the Plan of Salvation, she accepted Jesus, and joined the Family of God. Each Wednesday night at eleven o'clock and after the children were in bed, I would have Bible study with Amy in her mobile home.

After the second week, Amy said, "You know what, Coach? I am pregnant again," she said.

"So, you are pregnant, so what?" I countered.

"I don't want the baby," Amy informed me. "I already have five; I am going to have an abortion."

Now, I could have jumped to my feet and told her how I thought abortion was murder, and how God's Word indicated abortion is murder. But I didn't. I just said, "O.K., you are going to have an abortion, so what? I am not interested. Let's get into the scriptures."

Once again Amy read the scriptures out loud, and I discussed them with her and closed in prayer, and left.

Two months later, Amy said to me, "Coach, I am not going to have an abortion. I am going to give the kid away. Do you know anyone who will take it as soon as it is born? I don't even want to see it."

"So you are going to give the kid away, so what? I could care less. Let's get into the Bible and get to know Jesus better," I responded.

Once again, we completed our Bible study and closed in prayer.

About a month before the baby was to be born, Amy informed me, "Coach, I am not going to give my baby away. I love it, and I am going to keep it."

"O.K., you are going to keep your baby, so what? I could care less. Let's learn more about Jesus," I answered.

About a month after the baby was born, I took my wife to see it. As Amy held that cute little baby girl in her arms, I asked her, "Amy, aren't you glad that Jesus changed your mind?" and she smilingly nodded her head.

You see, friends, I could have told Amy that second night what she should have done or not done. All I would have accomplished was to turn her off, and she would have had the abortion. But as I encouraged her to read the Bible and pray, and as she became closer to Jesus, He changed her mind. Only God changes people. Amy has moved and the last I heard, she has been out of fellowship with her Lord. I continue to pray that God will bring her back, and I know He will answer my prayer.

What Happened To My Wife?

One night I received a call from Mary. "Coach, I have a girl friend down here and she is in a terrible predicament. I don't know what to tell her. Will you come down?" I agreed to go, even though it was one o'clock in the morning. Mary's girl friend had an eight year old daughter who had just been sexually molested by a teenage boy. Nancy was frantic, crying hysterically, "How can you help me?"

"There is only one way I can help you, and that is to introduce you to Jesus, and then He can help you." So at that early hour in the morning, Nancy accepted Jesus and became my sister in Christ.

The next morning my doorbell rang, and upon opening the door I saw Dick, Nancy's husband, who demanded, "I want to know what happened to my wife last night. I want to know what is going on around here?"

"Come on in, Dick," I said. "Here is a copy of God's Word. I want to tell you how you also can become a child of God, and reap all these benefits that Nancy is going to receive." Forty minutes later, Dick became my brother in Christ.

God Is Forgiveness

Darlene is a fine Christian girl, but her marriage disintegrated, ending in divorce. She lived alone with her only son. Darlene was trying to keep close to God, but she was having trouble, as her reactions to other people, including Christians, were setting up a barrier between her and Jesus. She was on the defensive concerning divorce. She knew what the Bible said about divorce, and it bothered her. Other Christian people, including ministers, continued to remind her of what the Bible said about divorce. Darlene was miserable, and found it unpleasant to attend church and other Christian activities in fear of what someone might say or think about her or how they might even look at her.

Being a close friend of the family, I started having Bible studies with Darlene, and God began to clear up the hangups she had. As we proceeded into the scriptures, I asked Darlene, "Were you a Christian when you were married?"

She said she was.

"Do you believe your marriage was a mistake?"

"Yes," she said.

"Have you asked God's forgiveness for this mistake, and have you been truly sorry for the mistake?"

Once again she said she was.

"Then according to the scriptures, Darlene, God has not only forgiven your mistake, He has also forgotten about it. You don't have to worry about what other people think, because you are right with your God. All He wants you to do now, is use these same guidelines about marriage for the future, and try to do better."

I also told Darlene about the woman caught in the act of adultery. Jesus came along and found people stoning a woman, and He asked them what they were doing. They told Jesus, "We are stoning her to death. She was caught in the very act of adultery. In fact, we saw her, and the law says she should be punished. We are right, aren't we?"

Jesus said, "Those without sin continue to throw the stones," and Jesus walked off. Returning to the woman, He said, "Where are your accusers, woman?"

She said, "They have all left, Lord."

Jesus answered, "I don't accuse you either, go and sin no more."

Jesus was telling her because she was truly repentant, that He had forgiven and forgotten her sin. Now she should use His guidelines to try and do better in the future.

It is always amazing to me how our Jesus can forgive and forget when we truly repent. Many times we as Christians refuse to forgive the same sin and the same person. Praise God, Darlene is now living close to God, and she has a happy, fruitful life in Jesus. She is happy because of a Wonderful Saviour, and one who does not only set up guidelines, but also forgives.

Slant Eyes

When I was overseas in World War II, I learned to hate orientals.

Even though I joined the Family of God when overseas, I still hated orientals. "Slant eyes", I once called them. Perhaps the films we saw portraying the atrocities committed by the Japanese, and the stories we heard had a lot to do with my ability to hate them. I detested not only the Japanese, but all orientals including the natives of Hawaii.

On my way home from Okinawa, we stopped at Honolulu. I was gypped by an oriental taxi driver, and that added fuel to the fire. When I was discharged, I was given back my job as a teacher and coach at Coldwater High School.

At the first teacher meeting, an elderly school teacher spoke up and suggested that we take an offering to purchase pencils for the Japanese school children.

I stood up, and 'blew my stack.'

I feel bad when I realize how much hate was in my heart.

When I started to read God's Word, pray to my God, and serve Jesus, the hate started to leave my heart, and now I love orientals.

A few years ago when I was in Kansas City at a Gideon International Convention, I invited two Japanese Gideons out for dinner, and also invited their interpreter.

The Japanese Gideons asked the interpreter to ask me my name.

I replied, "Eby, Eby, Eby."

One of the Japanese Gideons had a salad with a shrimp in it, and he pointed at the shrimp and said, "Eby, Eby, Eby."

The interpreter informed me that "Eby" is what they call shrimp in Japanese.

I came right back at the interpreter. "Where do they get that saying then about a little shrimp."

The Japanese Gideon answered through the interpreter, "Eby stands for lobster, also."

Japanese Gideons are not slant-eyed Japs any more to Floyd Eby, but brothers in Christ. And I love them. I have some special friends in Hong Kong now, who are my brothers and sisters in Christ. I correspond regularly with them since meeting them in Washington, D.C. God has now given me a special love for orientals. God took away the hate in my heart as soon as I started reading the Bible, praying to God, being with other Christians, and serving Jesus. Legislation and laws cannot do away with racial prejudice, but God can, and will, if we will surrender our lives to Him, and put Him first in our lives. I praise Him for making it possible to love everyone.

God Can Open A Door Through A Mistake

I was spending two days and nights in Detroit working for the Gideon Missionary Arm of the churches. Among many other names, I received Howard's name from a pastor as a Gideon prospect, but it was a mistake because Howard didn't even go to church. I was in a motel room calling prospects, and I had set ten o'clock as cut off time, so I wouldn't start getting people out of bed. At exactly ten o'clock for my last call, I tried Howard's number.

Howard's wife answered, and I asked her if her husband was home. She told me that he was at an A.A. meeting. I started to discuss the alcoholism problem with her, as well as other problems until she said, "You know, you sound like the type of man I would like to have talk to my husband."

I questioned her about the hour she expected him back, and she told me around ten-thirty. I told her if she wanted me to, I would come over. Howard was there by the time I reached his house.

I gave them Bibles and opened the scriptures, and went through the Plan of Salvation.

Then I told them how much I had needed to get close to God. Also I explained how I was growing spiritually every day, and how they could do the same, and our Lord would then take over their problems.

This was the starting of a fine friendship between Howard and Jane and Betty and Floyd Eby. I am sure we have helped each other get closer to God.

I praise God because we can never have too many brothers and sisters in Christ. We have visited each other several times and have gone to many Christian activities together.

* * *

You Are A Fanatic

At a school where I was teaching, my principal and I were eating together one noon in the cafeteria. He said, "Floyd, you are quite a religious fanatic. Do you believe everything in the Bible?"

"I sure do," I replied.

"Do you believe that story about the flood, Noah's Ark, and all those animals?"

"I sure do."

"How come?"

"Because it is in the Bible," I declared. "And that is good enough for me."

Several times over the years, my principal would bring up things about the Bible. Now I am happy to say that my former principal and his wife are two of my dear brothers and sisters in Christ. We belong to the same Gideon camp and meet in monthly camp meetings and fellowship together at a weekly prayer meeting and breakfast. I praise God that He could take two skeptics like me and my former principal and make believers out of us, and give us the sweet fellowship that we are now having as brothers in Christ.

Counting Up To Five

Lori accepted the Lord one night in a home Bible study, and she became on fire for Jesus in a "bubbly" way. She commenced going to two Bible studies each week, to church, and to all of the area evangelistic meetings. She would go forward to let everyone know she had been saved. However, her husband was stationed in Indianapolis, Indiana, while Lori worked in Coldwater, Michigan. Periodically, Lori's husband, Merle, would come to Coldwater on weekends. He was disturbed about this "Jesus Freak" movement, as he called it, that had done a snow job on his wife. He resented her new-found joy and told her so, but she continued to grow spiritually.

One weekend, Merle told Lori to either denounce this Jesus

Christ or he was going to leave her, because she couldn't love this Jesus and love Merle also. Lori told him that she could love him more, because she loved Jesus, but Merle wouldn't buy that. Merle came home on Easter weekend, and Lori and he engaged in a violent argument. Merle physically beat his wife. Merle blamed Coach Eby for Lori's new fanaticism. Lori left the house and went to a phone to call me. I picked her up with my car and left her at a motel where she was going to spend the night. On my way home, I decided to go meet Merle for the first time. Everyone had advised me not to do this because Merle resented me so much, even though he had never met me. But I thought it was time to meet him and talk with him about Jesus! I rang the doorbell. I guessed the man inside was Merle, and I rushed over to him and grabbed his hand and shook it, saying, "Merle, I am Coach Eby, and I am real glad to meet you. I came over to say hello, and get acquainted."

As soon as I mentioned the name of Coach Eby, Merle grabbed me by the collar with his left hand and clenched his right fist, and stuck it right up to my mouth.

He shouted swear words and obscene language and said, "I am going to count up to five. If you are not out of this house by then, I am going to shove your teeth right down your throat with my fist. Do you understand?"

He started counting, "One, two," and I interrupted. "Merle, I just want to talk to you." He continued, "Three, four," and on four, I left in a hurry.

When I got in my car and started home across town, something great happened to me. In spite of the swearing, obscene language, and the rude treatment I received, I felt no resentment against Merle. In fact, I loved him. I knew this had to be of the Lord, because no way could Floyd Eby help resenting such a guy and such treatment.

I praised God all the way home, and I thought, "Eby, it was your fault, not Merle's. It was not God's timing for you to stop to see Merle but your own mistaken timing." I asked the Lord's forgiveness for running ahead of Him. Arriving home around seven-thirty, I was working at my office desk waiting for a nine o'clock appointment to talk with a farmer and his wife and daughter about Jesus. The phone rang. The man said, "Eby, this is Merle, and first of all I want to apologize for being so rude."

I almost fell off my chair.

"But I want to tell you something, Eby, and I want you to listen," He said with profanity and vulgar language.

I interrupted, "Merle, I will listen to you one one condition. If when you are through talking, you won't hang up, but you will then listen to me. Otherwise, I will hang up on you right now."

"I have things to tell you," he replied, "And I will agree to that condition."

Then Merle went on to tell me how he thought I was clear out of place taking his wife away from him through this Jesus movement. He also said he was going to get even with me, and he knew how to do it. Also, he said he was going to kill Barry, another one of my home Bible Christians, who also knew Lori.

I told Merle I could understand why he could be so mad at me. I admitted it really was my fault, not his, because it was poor timing on my part in stopping to see him. He agreed it was terrible timing. Finally, he said, "You know, you don't sound like the kind of man that I thought you were."

"I hope not, Merle," I answered.

I then asked him if I could talk, and he agreed to that. I talked to him about my faith in God, and I asked him for his address in Indianapolis. He wanted to know why. I told him I was going to write him a letter. He said he wouldn't answer it, and I told him I didn't care, so he gave it to me. Then Merle said, "The only way this all wonderful, compassionate God of yours can prove Himself to me, is by bringing my wife back to me."

"I'll tell you, Merle, I can't speak for God or Lori. I don't know what God has in store for you and Lori. That's up to Him."

But Merle insisted the only way God could ever prove Himself to Merle was to bring Lori back to him.

Monday morning I wrote Merle a letter and mailed it to his

Indianapolis address. Monday night I heard that Lori and Merle went back together on Sunday, the day after I talked to Merle. They went back to Indianapolis together, Praise God. Merle received my letter about three days later, and I received an answer from Lori. She had located a fine young Christian couple and Merle like them very much. She believed Merle would soon accept the Lord. I was giving this testimony to one of my home Bible study groups one night, and Ted spoke up, "Coach, that was God's timing for you to stop and talk to Merle that night."

"What do you mean, Ted?" I asked. "Are you crazy; what would ever make you think that?"

"If it had been your timing instead of God's timing, Merle would not have counted to five, he would have just slugged you without counting!"

So, perhaps it was God's timing. Praise God that He works in all kinds of situations.

Who Has The Right To Tell Me?

One of my friend's daughters in her early twenties was living with a black man, a former college football player. The girl's parents naturally did not think much of this. Mary always confronted her parents with the question, "Who has the right to tell me what to do and what not to do?" The parents gave me Mary's and Mark's address where they lived in a large city, and asked me if I would stop in and talk with them.

I told my friends if God opened the door I would, but all I could promise was that I would try and make contact.

One day, I was driving through this city, and I happened to be on the right street and I stopped at the address. However, I was told they had moved. Several months later, I met the parents again, and they gave me the new address and also the telephone number. One night I called the number and Mary answered. "Mary, this is Coach Eby from Coldwater. Remember me?" She knew me even though I had not seen her since she was a small child. "You know, Mary, I am driving to your city on business tomorrow, and I am going to have an extra hour. I thought perhaps I could stop and chat with you, since I haven't see you for years. I am not going to preach to you or Mark, but I have found something that is great, and it is free, with no obligation. If you don't like what I say, you can turn me off quickly by saying so, and I will leave. What about it?" She agreed it would be fine with her. Mark was out of town.

Mary greeted me at the door and invited me in. "I don't have any Do's or Don'ts for you, Mary. I just want to tell you what happened to Floyd Eby, and what a wonderful life God has given me and my wife," I exclaimed.

With Mary reading the verses of scriptures, and me discussing them with her, Mary professed Jesus, and joined the Family of God. Mary said, "Mark is all mixed up in another religion, but he's starting to doubt it. How can I prove to him that this is the right one that can solve our problems and give us a happy, fruitful life?"

"It is simple, Mary, just tell him that when the leader of his so-called religion is killed, and is then raised from the dead three days later with all kinds of historical proof, then you will be interested. But now you already have Christianity that has completely met this test."

I have written Mary and talked with her on the phone. I am still attempting to make contact with Mark and will as soon as God opens the door. In the meantime, I pray for both of them, and Mary says she is praying for me, and she is reading the Bibles I gave her. Give me patience, dear Lord!

We Could Find No Answers

One night at ten-thirty, I received a telephone call at my home.

"Coach Eby, do you remember me? I am Sam."

"Yes, I remember the name, Sam." He had been one of my former students. "What can I do for you?" I asked.

"I am staying in Room 8 at the New Michigan Motel here on Division Street. I have problems. Would you come down and help me?"

I drove to the motel, and found the right door. Sam let me in, and then jumped back into bed.

Sam, a twenty year old lad, had been living in this motel room for three weeks with an eighteen year old girl, Dottie.

"Coach," he said, "For the last three days we have been shouting and screaming at each other, beating each other, scratching each other, and we just don't know what to do. I got out that blue Bible," he said. "And I told my girl friend Dottie that maybe this Bible had some answers for us. We tried reading it, but we couldn't understand it, and we could find no answers for our problems." Sam said he then took the blue Bible and placed it back on the dresser. As he laid it down, he saw the message, "Placed by the Gideons." "I just knew that you must be hooked to the Gideons and that you would help us with our problems, Coach. You can, can't you?"

"No, I am sorry, Sam and Dottie, but I cannot help you with your problems."

Sam and Dottie looked disappointed.

"However," I said, "I can tell you about Jesus Christ who can change your life completely, and take over all of your problems."

I opened that very same blue Bible, and told Sam and Dottie about Jesus, and they professed Jesus and joined the Family of God.

That weekend, Sam and Dottie moved out of that motel room, secured a minister and were married. They are now living in a home of their own with a beautiful baby daughter. I wish I could report to you that they no longer have problems. They have lots of problems, as the devil is still around, and both Sam and Dottie need to get closer to the Lord.

One night I received a telephone call from an irate Sam, who asked, "Coach, doesn't it say in the Bible that the man is the head of the house?"

I answered, "Sam, keep on reading the Bible, keep praying, be with other Christians, and serve Jesus, and I have to go to Bay City."

I knew Sam and Dottie were still having problems, but that

ONLY GOD CHANGES PEOPLE / 223

he also was reading the Bible. Praise God I had the privilege of placing that blue Bible in Room Eight.

What Would You Do If It Was Your Daughter?

Recently I received a telephone call from a couple in their fifties who wanted some counseling. I had worked a few months before with their daughter and son-in-law, who had many problems, but I had never talked to the parents, Bruce and Ruth, about Jesus. The daughter had informed me that her mother and father were also having trouble. I prayed about this meeting and decided I would approach Bruce and Ruth with God's Plan for their lives, before I asked them what they wanted of me. I rode my mini-bike to their mobile home and they invited me in.

After a few minutes of conversation about general things, I asked, "Would it be all right if we started this conference with me telling you two friends about a new way of life that my wife and I have found that has been so exciting as well as pleasant and wonderful?" Both of them agreed, but Bruce did say that they had some important questions to ask about their daughter's life and problems. I assured him that we would have time for that also. I presented two Bibles to each one, after writing in their names and my name. Then I presented God's Plan of Salvation, and told them what had happened to Floyd Eby when I joined the Family of God. It all made sense to Ruth, and she accepted Jesus, and joined the Family and became my sister in Christ. But Bruce had reservations, "I know there is a supreme being which could be called God, but my belief ends there."

I told Bruce that was his privilege, as our Lord gives everyone a free choice. "Ruth and I will pray that God reveals Himself to you like He has to both of us, and you can then also enter the Family," I revealed.

"Now, Floyd, what are we going to do about our daughter and son-in-law, and the type of life they are living?" Bruce wanted to know.

"You know, Bruce, I have worked with Lou Ann and Mike

for a year or more, and they both have accepted Jesus," I reminded him.

"It sure hasn't done much good," he answered.

I told Bruce that for a couple of months, Lou Ann and Mike had been reading the Bible, praying, having daily devotions, attending a weekly Bible study, and attending church weekly. God was blessing them by giving them jobs, and they were getting along better now than ever before on their own profession. It didn't last because both of them decided that everything was now strictly O.K., and they did not need God any more. As they quit growing spiritually, the troubles came back and increased. I have been praying for them regularly, and they come see me occasionally.

"You know, Eby, when we first met you, and you started helping our daughter, we were real suspicious of you," Bruce commented. "When you wouldn't accept any money, and donated your own time, and money, we just knew that you had some ulterior motive."

Ruth added, "We just knew something had to be wrong, because your compassion was too good to be true."

"I am going to tell you something, Eby, and it shouldn't make you mad," Bruce said. "Right after we met you, I investigated you thoroughly. I contacted seven prominent citizens and businessmen in this community, and had an individual conference with each one of them concerning Floyd Eby. Not one of them said anything about you except praise, and now I know that you are a good man."

"I am sorry, Bruce, but you must have contacted the wrong men, because Floyd Eby is not good. Floyd Eby is bad," I answered.

"That's not so, Eby," Bruce insisted. "You know that people know you are a good man."

"Bruce, the only part of Floyd Eby that is good, is the part that Jesus controls," I informed him. "Jesus living in me is good, but Floyd Eby is only good in the proportion that Jesus is controlling my life."

Bruce started talking about his daughter. He complained about how he had to pay a drug bill at the drug store for drugs

ONLY GOD CHANGES PEOPLE / 225

that Lou Ann needed to help her with her nerves and drinking. He had paid money to help her get her teeth fixed and paid up many of her back bills. All this time that lazy son-in-law was drawing unemployment and spending it on other things. How much more would he be expected to do? His daughter was humiliating him and his wife by the messy way she was living with this bum. Bruce's friends knew all about it, and it was downright embarrassing. The two of them smoke up three dollars worth of cigarettes every day and they don't make good use of the money they do have. Bruce said he was fed up with the whole situation.

"What would you do if she were your daughter?" Bruce asked.

"Bruce, I would love her to death," I answered. "The first thing I would do would be to get together with my daughter...alone. I would not criticize her husband or her way of living. I would tell her, 'Honey, I really love you, and no matter what happens, I am going to shower you continually with my love and compassion, and I am going to pray for you and your family every day.' Bruce, if I know your daughter, Lou Ann, she will throw her arms around you and cry with joy, because she needs your love."

Ruth spoke up. "That is just what Bruce ought to do and that is what Lou Ann needs. But he won't do it, and he's just got to do it."

"Listen, Ruth," I answered, "No way can you, nor should you, force Bruce to take this step. It will only be meaningful if Bruce does it from the heart."

Ruth continued, "I can't stand it any more unless our relationship with our daughter gets better, and Bruce has got to do it."

I reminded Ruth that she is now a child of God, and she should not use leverage on Bruce. If this relationship was causing her to get uptight, then she needed to get closer to God. "You see, Ruth, you and I need to pray for Bruce and Lou Ann and her husband, because Bruce cannot until he accepts Jesus as Saviour. Only God will change Bruce, Ruth, Lou Ann, Mike, or Floyd Eby. Bruce has been trying to change Lou Ann by helping her financially, and using pressure on her and Mike, but it won't work. It is a fact that people cannot change people; only God can change people. Let's pray that God will change all of our lives.

Bruce, Ruth, and I stood up and joined hands in a circle, and I prayed that God would reveal Himself to Bruce, and that He would also put Ruth, Mike, Lou Ann and me under conviction to discipline ourselves to read the Bible more; to pray more, to be with other Christians more, and to serve Jesus more.

This is the only way that our Lord will change our lives.

And we know that all things work together
for good to them that love God, to them who
are the called according to His purpose
Romans 8:28

15

GOD IS GOOD

In Romans 8:28, we find that Jesus can work everything out to our good if we love Him enough. Many times people ask me how that can be so, with all of these bad things continuing to happen. And I like to explain it in this way. Our grandmothers, when they baked a cake before the day of instant mix, would use all the separate ingredients such as butter, lard, flour, salt, yeast, and flavoring. All of these ingredients individually would not taste good. In fact, some of them would actually taste terrible. When grandmother mixed them all together into a delicious cake, it tasted wonderful, and this was the result of all these ingredients mixed together in the right proportion.

God can also take all of the bad things that happen to us, mix them together in the right proportions, and what comes out will be a wonderful, happy, fruitful life in Jesus. This is God's promise in Romans 8:28. And God is no liar. All we have to do to receive this promise as a Christian is to love Him enough, or put God first in our lives. We can then rest assured that our lives will turn out for the best for us.

In Everything Give Thanks

Ephesians 5:20 *Giving thanks always for all things unto God and the Father in the name of our Lord Jesus Christ.*

I flew to Petoskey one Sunday for a church service, and afterwards I flew into the upper peninsula to visit a young man who had accepted Christ while in jail, and had since been transferred to Camp Shingleton. I landed at a small grass strip between some woods, and about three miles south of a little village called Wetmore.

In order to get to Camp Shingleton, I knew I would have to go three miles north to Wetmore, and then ten miles east to reach the Camp. It was now two o'clock, and I knew visiting hours ended at the camp at exactly three-thirty, so I was anxious to get there as soon as possible.

I taxied my plane up near an old building and parked it. Getting out, I walked up to an elderly man standing outside and asked, "Do you have any cars for rent?"

He looked at me like I was crazy, and said, "Nope."

Of course, I knew he didn't have any rental cars, but I thought I might open the door for him to offer to take me to my destination, or perhaps let me rent his own car. But that door obviously remained shut.

I walked about a block to the blacktop going to Wetmore, and I started hitchhiking. When twelve cars passed me by within the first fifteen minutes, and all were going the wrong direction, I became somewhat discouraged. Finally, a car came along heading in the right direction and I put on my most honest face, a winsome smile, and stuck my thumb in the air.

However, he didn't stop, and I was just about ready to express my displeasure when I thought of Ephesians 5:20 of thanking God for all things.

"Thank you, God, for not stopping that car. I didn't want to ride with him anyway," I rationalized.

Another car came along and I could see before he reached me that he wasn't going to stop.

As I waved goodbye to him I said, "Thank you, Lord. He

didn't stop. Thank you, thank you. It is such a nice day and the flowers look so pretty along the road; it is a good day for walking. Thank you, Lord."

However, I knew it was too far and not time enough to walk thirteen miles and still visit Max.

A third car came by going toward my destination, and once again no luck. The occupants didn't even give me a look. "Thank you, Lord, that couple would have held me up probably."

By now I realized I was kind of talking out of both sides of my mouth. I really wanted to thank the Lord, but time was getting late, and I was becoming concerned.

A fourth car also passed me by, and I once again thanked the Lord, and sealed it with, "I really mean it, God."

In the fifth car was a young couple, and they pulled off the side of the road and stopped.

I opened the back door and got in, thanking the Lord and them at the same time.

Before he pulled out onto the road, the driver asked me where I was going, and I told him to Camp Shingleton.

"My wife and I passed you going the other way," he said. "We decided to turn around and pick you up and to take you anywhere you are going. So we will take you right to the camp."

I praise God, because He knows what He is doing.

You see, He knew that the other four cars probably would have let me off in Wetmore, and I would have been stuck there. But my Wonderful Saviour prepared the right car. Even though He had to turn it around, and have the occupants go out of their way to take me to a place where He would give me an opportunity to serve Him. Praise the Lord!

I arrived at Camp Shingleton just before three o'clock, and Max said, "Coach, we have only forty-five minutes. The guards never allow anyone to visit one second past three-thirty. I told Max we would make the best of our time. I opened the Bible and we went through the scriptures together, and prayed together.

But God wasn't through yet.

Can you believe that the guard allowed me to visit Max until four o'clock?

Do you know why? Because this same guard got off duty at four o'clock. He allowed me to visit until that time, so he could go out of his way to drive me back to my plane. This allowed me to arrive back home in time for evening church service.

Yes, we can thank a loving, compassionate, all knowing, and powerful God for all things, because He always has everything under control.

Tell Me Where I Can Find Out About Jesus

I received a telephone call from a Gideon from a southern Michigan city. "Floyd, we have been trying to have a Gideon message in this certain church for the last twelve years. Now we have the opportunity, because their new pastor hasn't arrived as yet, and they are still using guest preachers. Two weeks from this Sunday, they have been unable to schedule a minister. Therefore we can send a Gideon speaker for the entire speaking time, thirty minutes. Will you take it for us?

I really wanted to turn it down, because I knew of this church. No way were they interested in what the Lord would have me say. I thought I could attend my own little home church for a good Bible message, and some sweet Christian fellowship with my own people.

But before I turned it down, I thought perhaps it was God's open door. I didn't want to miss any door God had opened, and I decided I would make sure by going -- just in case God wanted me there.

A few days later, my friend called me again, and stated that the church had now been able to secure a guest preacher, and had cut my time to five minutes.

The Gideon had talked them into giving me ten minutes.

Time doesn't really make any difference. I will go anywhere Jesus wants me to go for any amount of time. The cutting of the time only verified what I knew all along. The church really didn't want me, and would be happy to have me cancel out.

I decided to go over and suffer through the assignment. Between Sunday School hour and the Worship Hour we had a coffee break and some fellowship. The chairman of the Board of Deacons explained, "You know at one time I was a fundamentalist, believing every part of the Bible. But I ran into a minister who told me how to live with the Bible and these so-called miracles. Now I only believe that part of the Bible that is practical and makes sense, and no longer do I have trouble with such things as these so-called miracles. I just ignore them."

The guest preacher spoke first, and I heard one of the best lectures I ever heard on stream pollution and air pollution.

It actually made me sick when I realized how much those people out front needed the Word of God. I praise God that I had the last ten minutes to give them the Gospel.

After the service was dismissed, the chairman of the Board of Deacons and the guest minister went out on the outside porch near the front door to greet the people. I went across the porch on the other side to keep out of the way. People streamed out shaking the Deacon's and Guest Preacher's hands. I could hear many of them praising the minister for his wonderful message on such an important subject. Once in awhile someone would come over and shake my hand, and thank me for coming.

A tall young man came out of the church and shook both of their hands. He came over to me and shook my hand and said, "I appreciate your message about the Bible this morning. I have nothing against soil conservation, but I would like to know more about this Jesus you were talking about. I am a college student from Connecticut. Could you direct me to a church where I can learn more about this Jesus you are so sold on?"

I turned my back to the Deacon and the preacher and quietly asked this young man, "What is your name?"

"My name doesn't matter. I just want to know where I can find out more about Jesus."

Once again I asked, "Just give me your name, and I will see that you are taken care of."

"My name is Rex." I thought to myself, the Gideons haven't been in this church for twelve years, and here I am directing traffic to other churches. When I got home, I called a Gideon friend in that city.

"Gale, tomorrow morning you go down to the college and look up a Rex Jones, and tell him where he can go to church in your city to learn about Jesus."

Gale did better than that. He looked up Rex and invited him to his own church and then to Sunday dinner at his home.

Three weeks later, Gale's church had a series of revival meetings and on the second night, big Rex marched down the aisle, accepted Jesus as his Saviour, and he joined the Family of God. As the revival continued, Rex brought other college students.

Oh, how I think how close I came to turning God down on this assignment. God was interested in using me as a messenger, and I almost told Him I wasn't willing. I have learned not to try to out-guess my Lord!

Brother Gale told me that Rex after his freshman year, went to Europe to study, and he and his wife would hear from Rex occasionally. Three years later, Brother Gale passed away and went home to be with the Lord. I went to Brother Gale's church to attend his funeral, and as I walked out of the church afterwards, I noticed a large man. I walked up to him and said, "Sir, I have to ask your name."

"You are Floyd Eby, aren't you?" he asked.

"Yes, and you are Rex Jones," I replied.

Rex told me he had stopped in Coldwater to see me, but didn't find me at home. He had studied in Europe for two years, then returned to finish his senior year where he started. I asked him what he was going to do after graduation, and he said he was going into the ministry full time.

I met Rex again on the college campus while handing out testaments. Rex is now working full time in the ministry of "HIS Mansion" in Connecticut, a farm where problem youth come to learn about Jesus.

Praise God for the opportunity of being used by Him!

* * *

I was sent to a certain church in the state, on an assignment by the State Assignment Committee. The church had been particular in letting Gideon speakers in. The Gideon contact man had finally succeeded in securing a fifteen minute service on Wednesday prayer meeting night.

Being a touchy situation, the state committee had decided to assign the state Gideon President to this service.

I didn't really want to go, because it came on the same night as my five home Bible studies. But I made the necessary arrangements. I called the pastor, as we always do, to check details and let him know who was coming.

Pastor, I am Floyd Eby, the Gideon speaker assigned to your church a week from Wednesday night," I informed him.

"I don't want you," he replied.

"Sir, could you tell me why?" I asked.

"I am getting tired of you long-haired speakers with beards, red shirts, and polkadot ties standing in my pulpit. I have the Gideon I want, VanDyke. I know what he is like."

"Pastor, I will have to call the state committee, and find out about this, and I will call you back," I countered.

When I got the state director of speaker development on the phone, he told me he was sure VanDyke wasn't planning to take the assignment; that he had just secured the service. He directed me to take the assignment.

In the meantime, VanDyke had called the pastor, and told him he would be there on that Wednesday night to speak.

The pastor jumped him. "Well, then I am going to have two of you, because a guy by the name of Floyd Eby from Coldwater is going to be here, too."

VanDyke told him if Floyd Eby was coming that he wouldn't, and let it go at that.

I called the pastor back and told him that the state director had officially assigned me to his church at that time. The pastor didn't say anything about VanDyke having called him, but started in on me again about long hair, colored shirts, beard, and mod ties.

I interrupted him. "Pastor, my wife and I will show up Wednesday night and if you don't like the looks of either of us, we will sit in the front pew, and listen to you preach all night."

"All right. On that basis, you can come," he said.

Betty and I introduced ourselves to the pastor, and I asked him if fifteen minutes was the right amount of time allotted to me. I knew if the assignment committee was wrong, and it was only ten minutes and I spoke for fifteen, we would be in serious trouble.

The pastor answered. "We don't pay much attention to time around here."

"Do you expect to speak before I do, or after I do?"

"I am not going to speak at all," he said. "If you bring us something from the Word, you can have the entire time."

"How much time is that, pastor?" I asked.

"We don't pay much attention to time around here," he said once again.

There were about one hundred people there with lots of teenagers and children. I could tell that the pastor ran a tight ship, because I heard one of the Deacons say to the associate pastor, "Say, Wayne, isn't it about time you got a haircut?"

"Yeh," Wayne answered. "I don't dare wait much longer."

It sounded like me controlling my basketball players.

The service was turned over to me just after eight o'clock, and I spoke until eight-thirty, closing in prayer. I stepped down from the platform, and sat in the front pew. The pastor then conducted a forty minute altar call, with many committed people.

After this, the pastor came down on the main level in front of the pulpit, folded his arms and said, "Now we have had a good message tonight, and the speaker was well-dressed and looked very appropriate. We are going to take an offering for the Gideons, and we are going to give one hundred dollars. You can start bringing it up here now, and I will count it, and when we get one hundred dollars, we will quit."

I prayed, Lord don't let us stay here all night, because I know most of the audience is young people.

It was really quite moving to see small children with their

pennies and nickels, teenagers with their dimes and quarters, and the adults with their folding money laying it down on the platform in front of the pastor who was rapidly counting it. After three or four minutes, a lady in the third row back of me spoke up, "How much do you have now, preacher?" "Ninety six dollars and forty eight cents," he answered. "I will take care of the rest of it," she replied. "Stop," he said, "That is it." My wife and I thoroughly enjoyed that service, and this church which is such a fine spiritual church. I don't want the above unusual procedure to detract from the spirituality of this church. We praise God for churches and pastors like these!

Follow-up On Spiritual Children

I believe as God gives us the opportunity to be used of Him to see someone enter His Family, we should consider them as our spiritual children. We then have the responsibility of continuing as much as possible to encourage them to grow spiritually, to get closer to God, or get to know Him better and better, or get them to become a real close friend of Jesus, or to increase their faith, or to put God first in their lives. You see, as the one whom our Lord uses to bring a child of God into His Family, we are the best contact of anyone to encourage him to make this experience become real in his life. We have no right under God to shun this responsibility, or to turn it over to someone else -- unless to accept the assignment is an impossibility.

I immediately give each person two Bibles, a King James New Testament and a copy of a paraphrase of the Living Bible New Testament. I then follow-up with a letter, and ask the persons if they have signed the profession and recorded the date in the back of the little testament to indicate that they joined the Family of God that day.

I answer all letters I receive, writing each one as a personal letter in my own handwriting. I remind them of the four things they have to do to grow spiritually, and I ask them if they are growing spiritually.

I always ask for personal pictures of each person for my prayer board, and ask them to write and tell me about themselves and their families. I tell them if they want me to talk with their friends about Jesus, I will fly if possible to meet with them. I always tell them that I pray for them regularly, and I ask them to please pray for me. I also call long distance occasionally, and whenever possible when I am in the area, I call. I try to visit them, sometimes individually and sometimes in groups. I always call them in advance of the visit.

Sometimes, older people meet me at airports, and I spend thirty to sixty minutes reading the scriptures and praying with them. I try to combine the visits with speaking engagements in the same area, and sometimes I invite them to my speaking engagements, and we meet before or afterwards.

I keep a large address book with the names of all of my spiritual children, including their addresses, phone numbers, and ages.

I put these on my permanent prayer list, divided into the days of the week. Sure, this takes time, ambition, compassion, and money. But it pays real dividends.

I receive some of the sweetest letters ever. It is an exciting time every day when the mail comes, to see who I am hearing from this day; to see where the letter is from.

I sometimes write over one hundred personal letters in a week, and I am always behind. But praise God for all the prayer support I receive.

My relationship with Jesus is getting sweeter every day. Praise God!